MY WARWICKSHIRE WARTIME

1939 – 1945

GILL EMETT THOMAS

Published by Bombus Broom 2013
107 Henslow Road
Ipswich
IP4 5EJ

Illustrations by Rowland Emett

I have included four of my Uncle's drawings in this book: three cartoons and one illustration. After making enquiries I was unable to discover who owns the copyright to these works. Therefore I wish to acknowledge the sources of these drawings which I found in the following publications:

1   Cartoon page 12
     Reproduced from: *Rowland Emett,* published by Chris Beetles Ltd, 1988

2   Cartoon page 40
     Reproduced from: *Alarms and Excursions,* published by John Murray, 1977

3   Illustration page 53
     Reproduced from *Bells and Grass,* published by Faber & Faber, 1941

4   Cartoon page 82
     Reproduced from *Alarms and Excursions,* published by John Murray, 1977

I would be happy to remunerate any publisher or person who can prove copyright of my Uncle's drawings.

The map on page iii is a detail from a larger map published in 'Warwickshire' by Vivian Bird, 1973, by permission of Patrick Leason.

This book is dedicated to my cousin, Norma, who shared days with me at Halford, Tredington, Stratford and Henley during the war. She died in 2013 just as this book was completed, having been a generous and loving friend to my entire family.

Norma Goodenough in 1941

This map shows the villages of Halford and Tredington where
I lived with grandparents, and the little town of
Henley in Arden where I lived at Buckley Green Farm with
my parents through the time I was a boarder at the
Croft School, Stratford on Avon.

MY WARWICKSHIRE WARTIME
by Gill Emett Thomas

Contents

Granny Emett's cottage at Halford

Halford 1939

The Second World War broke out when I was seven years old. I wandered into the kitchen one Sunday morning to find my parents and a visiting uncle looking worried. They were talking about a war starting soon. What this meant exactly was not very clear to me but I was surprised to find that the result of this discussion was that I was going to live with Granny Emett for some time.

As I had never been away from home, except for a short and unhappy visit to hospital to have my tonsils out when I was four and a half, this was something of a shock. However, when I found that my best friend Jean was coming with me I felt much better.

Jean lived in the same road in Hall Green, Birmingham. Our pram pushing mothers had become friendly when we were babies and we were inseparable, attending infant school together and playing together every day.

We went off without much demur, reassured by the promise of frequent visits from our parents who would drive down to see us in the country. Granny Emett lived in an old stone cottage at Halford, not far from Shipston on Stour, on the edge of the Cotswolds.

Those first few days at Halford were quite a surprise. When we woke in the morning instead of washing and dressing ourselves we had to submit to Granny's ministrations. She energetically scrubbed our faces with a flannel and dried us equally roughly. This seemed an indignity to us. Perhaps Granny had forgotten what young children could do for themselves. After a day or two we must have convinced her that we could manage on our own.

Granny was altogether more vigorous than my mother and was brisk in anything she undertook. She was also kind and lively, and Jean and I felt welcome. We enjoyed looking round our new home inside and out.

Granny's cottage was built of golden Cotswold stone as were the church and most of the village houses. The cottage fronted the village church. On the left was a small row of cottages and the road which led down to the mill. In front of the little garden's iron railings was a verge where goats were sometimes tethered to crop the grass.

Inside its passages were cool and dark. In the living room one mullioned window in the thick stone wall looked over 'Granny's field' which sloped down to the river. There was quite a large garden at the side and back of the cottage where there was an old well with a handle for winding up buckets of water.

Entering a door from the garden at the back of the cottage we discovered a long low ceilinged room called the washhouse. There was a large copper for heating water for washday and stored lumber of various kinds. The old whitewashed interior smelt sweetly of apples stored and laid out on wooden trays on a part of the floor. There was also a black painted wooded shed for storing gardening implements, coal and kindling.

Nasturtians grew in the tiny strip of front garden and Granny showed us how to find and eat their peppery green seeds. Half coconuts were hung up on the rustic trellis for garden birds to eat.

All the furniture seemed ancient and uncomfortable compared to the soft seats at home. The sofa and two large armchairs were very hard and lumpy, although there was a basket weave chair that creaked loudly that I grew to enjoy.

On the left hand side of the front door as you entered Granny's cottage was the door to a long narrow room which ran from front to back of the cottages. It was cool and quiet. It was rarely entered or used, all life being centred round the living room or kitchen. There was a rather mysterious pianola with special rolls to insert which produced mechanical music. There were also books of Little King cartoons which I often looked at. Perhaps most significantly there was a bureau and in some of its drawers were stored my Uncle Fred's oil paints and brushes. The delicious smell of oil paint attracted me so much that I vowed silently to myself that I would use oil paints myself one day.

The main feature of the living room was the fireplace. This had a high mantle over a black leaded range where there was usually a fire burning. Various brass trivets and fire irons were displayed in front. I can remember the range's oven door being opened to take out the weekly joint and the delicious smell of roast meat.

The kitchen was quite small and there didn't seem to be any sort of oven. I think Granny cooked things on a little paraffin stove in there. There was a big cupboard, a larder I suppose, and ironing went on there.

One room was always light and sunny, that was Granny's bedroom which looked out over the garden at the back of the cottage. Here, on Granny's dressing table, were silver backed hair brushes where Granny brushed her pretty hair and little fringe. Vi slept in a larger darker room under the eaves at the front.

Vi was my Granny's 'companion', cheerful and energetic. She was strong with black hair and a wide smile. She often seemed to be smiling or laughing and was very good to Jean and I. Once I remember asking my mother who Vi was. My mother said that Granny had met her when Vi was working in a greengrocers shop, which didn't shed much light on the matter. Several years previously, when my Granny lived near to us in Birmingham, she had nursed my Grandfather Emett through his last illness. He died two years before I was born. After his death Granny decided to go and live in Halford – I believe the Emetts had rented holiday cottages there in previous summers so the villages were familiar. She must have offered Vi a position as companion at that point. Granny would have been in her early sixties and Vi perhaps in her late thirties. They both loved the country and were keen on long walks. There was no doubt that they enjoyed life in Halford.

Granny and Vi were both very energetic and active unlike my mother and her mother Granny Goodenough who were more gentle and comfort loving.

Jean and I enjoyed this new village life and were made very welcome by Granny and Vi. We knew this situation was not going to be permanent and explored our new world with enthusiasm.

At home in Birmingham we often went with our mothers to the local shops. These consisted of a recently built 30's row with a fishmongers, greengrocers, butchers and grocers among others.

At Halford there didn't at first appear to be any shops. Then we discovered a pretty old cottage with a bow window which was the sweet shop with very large glass jars holding boiled sweets. We rarely seemed to go there and I don't think we had any pocket money. We soon found out where all the action was. Granny went almost daily to 'Mrs Trenthams'. This was a long large shed opening at one end onto the main through road. Here a rather casual arrangement of stock of all kinds was laid out. Mrs Trentham, a dark haired vigorous lady, presided. She seemed to keep up a barrage of loud and knowing remarks to or about her customers. Even though Jean and I couldn't understand their meaning, their impact seemed caustic.   Here we were often bought an ice cream by Granny.   These were early Lyons ice creams, cylinders of hard yellow ice cream in a wrap of paper which was peeled off for the cylinder to be inserted in the ice cream cone.   We loved them.   Here too we were sometimes offered sherbet with a liquorice stick.   The sherbet tickled our noses and we were never sure if we liked this or not.

I don't remember seeing a butchers shop anywhere, maybe meat or fish were delivered.   I do remember Mr Biles and his weekly visits when he came to deliver groceries from his shop at Ettington.   He would come in while Granny checked the contents of the box and paid him.   He delivered to people over a wide area and regaled Granny and Vi with news of various 'goings-on' picked up on his travels.   He wore a brown overall and behind his glasses his eyes seemed to me to be both astute and knowing.

I loved the shoe repairers shop, it seemed so snug, complete and self-contained.   It was like a big garden shed, set on the tarmac path behind the main road.   Inside was a cheerful pleasant elderly man surrounded by all the tools of his trade.   It was always satisfying to make a visit there.   Children are always aware without anything being said, if they are welcome or not.   It always felt comfortable at the shoe menders.

Opposite to his shed, on the other side of the road, was a small square building made of cob, with a thatched roof.   On benches round the outside of this ancient building old men with their dogs would gather, smoke pipes and watch the world go by.   At intervals they would rise slowly and walk off with their equally arthritic dogs just about keeping pace.   I dimly realised, even from my little experience of life, that these chats and meetings gave them great satisfaction.

There was a large grand Cotswold manor house, it was not old and mellow like so many of the village buildings, but fairly modern, although built in traditional style.   Its stones were sharp edged and hard compared to the soft weathering of many of Halfords walls.   I didn't like it.

We once saw the lord of the manor riding a beautiful horse along a nearby boundary hedge.   He was tall, spare and aristocratic looking.   His face had a bluish tinge – I had heard of 'blue blood' and found this quite as expected.   At a local horse show we saw one of his sisters riding side-saddle ... she looked elegant and forbidding.   Snatches of overheard gossip fuelled the impression I had that happenings at the manor were well known in the village and reported around.   I once heard scandalised relish at the fact that 18 eggs had been used to make omelettes for guests at the manor.   This at a time when food was fairly sparse for all.

I remember little of the meals at Granny Emetts, except that she had some 30's style bowls decorated brightly with parrots in green, orange and black.   We were always given jelly in these plates and eagerly ate it up so that we could see the parrots at the bottom.

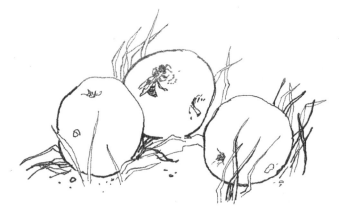

We must have enjoyed the weekend roasts as meat and gravy was possibly my favourite food at that time.

During these first weeks the apples on the fruit trees in Granny's field were ripening. We would look for ones to eat that had fallen into the soft grass. Warned by Vi we would look carefully for wasps before picking them up. This field always seemed to be full of golden sunshine which must be a distorted memory. It sloped down to the river Stour, a lovely small river with steep sandy banks, reeds and quacking ducks, bordered by pollarded willows.

Vi would take us to shallow water where the river widened by Halford bridges. Here she would supervise us fishing for minnows. Feeling tickles round our bare feet and ankles we would look down astonished to see tiny fish nibbling us. We had nets and jam jars with string handles and loved these excursions. We always tipped our catch back into the water at the end of the afternoon.

The lane outside the cottage led down to Halford Mill. Here lived a fierce family with an equally fierce dog named Spider. He was given to much loud barking with stiff legged jerking on the spot. He once chased me to the metal fence at the top of the lane where I clung to the top crying until Vi rescued me.

The large old pub around which much village life revolved was called the Bell. We never went in, just sometimes glimpsed its cool beer smelling interior and recognised that it was the hub of the village without knowing why.

Jean and I loved to play in the churchyard. To one side of the little entrance gate there was a quiet raised area up some steps and a small grassy area of gravestones. In the wall was a niche, a plaque and often fresh flowers. Here we would sit and play and talk together. No one ever seemed to mind. It seemed a pretty, romantic place to us and we went there often. We often went inside the church too. It had a door which closed with a clicking latch. We particularly liked looking at the pictures in a huge bible there. One very graphic engraving of Samson pulling down the pillars of the Temple gave Jean nightmares. I was too busy admiring the skills of the engraver to be much upset by the often frightening scenes.

Halford Church

Once we came upon a horse being shod at the picturesque village smithy. Our attention was drawn by a very peculiar smell and we drew near with a certain amount of trepidation. The insides of the smithy doors now pushed open wide by the blacksmith were covered in the leathery remains of small animals nailed to its surface. This made us uneasy to start with. A group of men stood around a placid brown cart horse. Then, to our amazement, the blacksmith picked up a heated horse shoe with tongs and clapped it onto the horse's uplifted foot which was braced onto his knee. As the hot metal hit the horse's hoof there was a slight sizzling sound, a wisp of smoke and a pungent sickening smell of burning. We were horrified. It seemed like a form of torture to us. We were astonished by the lack of reaction to this disgusting event by the horse. Feeling rather pale we went home to Granny. Here it was explained to us that it didn't hurt the horse – it was the same as having our nails or hair cut which did not hurt us at all if done carefully. We felt rather foolish.

Granny's cottage looked out towards Halford church and a group of cottages where the Webbs lived and there was a little gate leading down to the dairy at Lomas's farm.

At first Vi would take us to get the milk and then sometimes we would go on our own.

We would walk along a stone path beside the old farmhouse and then enter a door of the dairy which was a large cool room with slate shelves all round. The villagers had their own individual jugs there which were filled ready for them with cool milk. I think I once saw butter churning going on there too. I liked the dairy and enjoyed fetching the milk – little bantam hens were pecking about outside. I suppose Granny paid for the milk at the end of the week.

The Lomas's seemed quite elderly to me - Mr Lomas was a handsome man who usually wore a cream smock and a farmers hat and often carried two buckets from a yolk on his shoulders. Mrs Lomas was large and slow moving. They had a red-faced son called Percy and a daughter Ruth. If we saw Ruth Vi always chatted to her and asked to see her dolls. Ruth looked grown up to me but played with her dolls as though she was about eight or nine, and knitted them numerous clothes.

The Lomas's had a large wooden summer house in their garden and on Sundays large black cars would drive down our quiet lane decanting portly passengers in black. They all attended some sort of religious meetings at the farm, sometimes in the summer house I believe. Granny and Vi seemed to regard these meetings with some scepticism ...

Aunty Vi loved being with children which was a lucky bonus for us. Looking back I think she took us out each day after lunch so that Granny could have a rest. Without her life would have been much less fun.

Vi was never too busy to be interested in us. She listened intently to whatever we told her or asked her and seemed pleased to be with us. She took us out on walks round the village and its environs and particularly over in 'the park'. Walking through the churchyard and past pretty cottages on the left and the right we would make for a small path beneath a giant walnut tree. This path led via fences, styles and field tracks into the countryside and eventually the woods of Ettington Park.

Vi told us the names of the trees and the wild flowers. If we stung ourselves on nettles she showed us how to rub the stings with cool dock leaves. We found out how to loop the stalk of sorrel over itself to shoot off the rusty sorrel heads and how to look for burrs to throw at each others jerseys and coats (but not in the hair where their tiny hooks stuck fast so fiercely they sometimes had to be cut out). She taught us to recognise deadly nightshade and other poisonous plants. For part of our walk we looked down through elder bushes to where the river curved and meandered below us. Vi took us to a large fallen tree, leafless and bleached, its grey trunk and branches shaped like an aeroplane. We would climb about it pretending to be flying or landing our giant 'bomber'.

She showed us how to cut short lengths of elder twigs, poke out the soft pith inside and then cut notches in these short hollow lengths to make whistles. It is really only now, on writing about our time in Halford that I realise how much she showed us and taught us.

Vi was known and liked in the village. She must have sometimes collected Mr Lomas's cows for milking long before we arrived – now we went along to help her. We walked to a field back over the bridge and opened a gate where the cows were already waiting for us. They then ambled over the bridge, up the rise past the Bell, turned left and down to the entrance to the farmyard – a collection of barns grouped round a central dung heap. I think Jean and I had sticks and certainly felt important. However the cows could have made this daily journey in their sleep and really didn't need us, just someone to open and close gates. All this rural life was very satisfying – a far cry from riding our tricycles and fairy cycles in Birmingham.

After a while it was arranged that Jean and I should go to the village school. We were a bit frightened at playtimes by the rough playing of some of the village boys wearing big boots and their noisy tussling and rough games. However, they meant us no harm and we grew used to them.

Inside the sunny big room of the school we sat near to each other. We were surprised to find that after dinner-time each day the youngest children were put down to have a nap. Little folding canvas beds were put along the side of the room and the baby children would sleep under a blanket each. When they were woken they looked like dazed little owls, blinking and drowsy. My memories of the lessons are vague except for some enjoyable singing and marching round the piano.

One great delight was the making of raffia mats. We were given a piece of card with a framework of fine string attached to one surface. Then we could choose shiny raffia in brilliant colours to weave round and round until our mats were made. The choice of colours was left to us to select and combine ourselves. I enjoyed this so much I can vividly remember it. I think we could even take our mats home.

One less happy occasion was when all the children had a compulsory session with a visiting woman dentist who came to the school. I didn't feel particularly apprehensive as I'd visited our own dentist back in Hall Green. It was a shock to have to endure some brisk and painful drilling of my teeth. Most children cried.

Jean and I continued to enjoy our walks with Vi and our explorations of the village.

Once, visiting the farmyard where I remember being fascinated by the sweet smelling shiny brown pellets of cattle cake in hessian sacks, we saw a large rat. Being totally inexperienced in country life, and not realising that rats in farmyards were common place, we thought this was a momentous event. Rats in our story books were always sinister and up to no good. I crouched down to corner the rat who crouched opposite me – its eyes looked reddish with glittering pin points of light. Jean ran to get Mr Lomas. The rat began to gather itself as if to make a spring. Mr Lomas arrived with his gun, gestured to me to move aside, shot the rat, lifted it by the tail and flung it on the dung heap. All this was done very calmly – no recriminations were made and he allowed us to go home feeling we had accomplished something of moment. A generous hearted man.

After war was declared our parents had expected bombing and fighting to take place at once. Many children were evacuated into the country which is why we were sent to Halford. I believe that little happened for several months, a period that came to be nicknamed 'the phoney war'.

At about this time my mother's parents, Granny and Grandpa Goodenough, decided to move down to Warwickshire too. Selling their house in Hall Green, they bought a large bungalow on the edge of Tredington village nearby. As it was now decided that my mother and father and I would be moving to live with them, Jean went back to Hall Green to her parents.

Our stay with Granny Emett had always been visualised as a short-term arrangement. When Jean left I missed her, but to compensate there were frequent visits from my parents and grandparents until the move was finalised and I knew I would go to Tredington too.

In the meantime Granny and Vi taught me to knit, perhaps in case I was lonely without Jean. Vi and Granny were expert knitters. Long before everyone took to knitting as a way to eke out clothes coupons they had been knitters. Now in the war time their knitting became more enthusiastic than ever. They liked wooden buttons and earth colours of russet, mustard, brown and green ... they were particularly good on heavy jackets and also knitted me fair-isle jumpers in thinner wool. When they taught me how to knit I enjoyed it, provided I could make scarves or simple things. After learning how to cast on, to plain and purl I remember a very satisfying plump stitch called moss stitch that I loved. Because of wartime economies sometimes people used to unpick old knitted garments to re-knit them into new ones.

Now that it was getting darker earlier, each evening Granny and Vi would settle by the fireside with their knitting. Their ancient high backed wing chairs were padded with cushions and covered by faded throws. The beautiful paraffin lamp with its tall glass funnel was lit and cast a gentle radiance over the two knitters. The fire in the range creaked and shifted and sometimes let down a little fall of ash. Their feet rested on a rag rug and Sam the black cat was allowed to curl up in the warmth. A thick curtain was pulled across the door and the draught beneath blocked by a long knitted and padded 'sausage'.

I particularly remember one evening when I sat just outside the radiant pool of light colouring a picture for a children's colouring competition, taking immense care. To my chagrin next morning's daylight showed that all the objects that I thought I had crayoned brown, were in fact purple. For the first time I learnt that artificial light altered colours. Granny told me that Fred had special 'daylight' light bulbs for doing artwork at night.

Fred was my father's younger brother, an artist, tall and fair and good looking. When I saw him, which was not often, he was always nice to me. When I was very young he had painted me a most satisfying picture for my bedroom wall beside my cot. The picture showed two friendly elephants sitting on a rug. The delicious way the soft grey watercolour paint for the elephants had been applied to the thick watercolour paper delighted me.

I looked intently at any of Uncle Fred's pictures owned by the family. My parents had a watercolour of a house among trees, my Goodenough grandparents had an oil seascape, my cousin Norma's parents had an oil of willow trees and there was a painting of Halford church next to the paraffin lamp by the fireside corner of Granny's cottage.

"She just says she does this cove EVERY year"

One of Uncle Fred's wartime cartoons for Punch magazine

Later, during the war, Fred became famous as the cartoonist, Emett of Punch magazine. He used his middle name and was now called Rowland Emett. I loved the fine lines and details of his cartoons which all related to wartime shortages and problems of every kind. I remember some years later reading an article about him in an American magazine. The Americans took to his quirky take on eccentric English characters in a big way.

I remember that during my time at Halford he came for short visits. Early one morning I saw him gathering his easel and paints ready to go and paint out of doors. I asked if I could go with him and was very disappointed when he said no. I realise now that it would have been impossible for him to work down by the river with a small girl exploring nearby – but I was sad at the time.

Neither my father or Fred were in the forces unlike so many other men at the time. My father had an incipient stomach ulcer which kept him from joining up, although he later joined the local Observer Corps. Fred was employed on aircraft design after an earlier career before the war in a commercial studio. One of my mother's brothers, Uncle Eric, was in the Pioneer corps while his elder brother, Ralph, continued to run their family business in Birmingham which supplied metal components needed for the war effort. He was also involved with the wartime auxiliary fire service.

Granny's cottage adjoined a smaller much older cottage named Thatchcot which had very thick stone walls and a thatched roof. Here lived Aunty May and Miss Sutton. Perhaps they told Granny when the next door cottage became vacant so that she and Vi could move in. Aunty May was actually my father's aunt and so I suppose was Granny's sister-in-law, a fact which did not occur to me at the time.

May was about sixty in these days, small and agile with a quite severely bent back. I remember her face as being gentle, vague and kind. Miss Sutton was taller and larger, possessed of the power and authority associated by me with headmistresses. She used a stick and suffered very badly with arthritis. She was always pleasant and often humorous but the capacity for critical attack seemed always present. Some time previously I believe Miss Sutton ran a rather select boarding house in Bournemouth where Aunty May was employed by her. Now they had retired to Halford where Aunty May was Miss Sutton's companion. Even at my age I think I realised that this meant Aunty May did most of the menial work.

I found the inside of Thatchcot fascinating. The dark living room had a small padded window seat in the thickness of the wall where I liked to sit to survey my surroundings. It was rather smart in the manner of a previous age. The very dark furniture, almost black, was highly polished as were pieces of silver or brass. There were bowls of sweet scented pot-pourri and watercolours with wide gold mounts inside their narrow frames. Books with limp suede covers graced the bookshelves.

I once had to go upstairs for some reason and saw to my amazement that one of the central beams holding up the roof was actually an ancient tree, blackened by time and not trimmed into a regular shape. The cottage was reputed to be very old and I had heard a story that it was some sort of staging post for travellers on horseback taking message for Henry VIII. I should think this highly unlikely, but I liked the story.

Along the length of the back wall of the cottage a roofed in glass conservatory had been built. It was sunk beneath the level of the garden and was very sunny and sheltered. I remember many plants and basket-chairs and 'everlasting' flowers hanging up to dry in bunches from the roof. I think these were used to make the pot-pourri. The garden was mainly grass, with a sweet smelling camomile lawn and some paving stones. This garden was bounded on the far side by a stone wall beyond which could be seen the end of the village school. An ancient alleyway ran between the two. On the near side, next to Granny's garden, there was just a fence and I would sometimes look past Granny's fruit trees and currant bushes to see 'Miss Suttons ladies' having afternoon tea on the lawn.

I suppose these ladies, who seemed to appear in the summer time could have been guests at the Bournemouth boarding house in the past. They intrigued me. I was not used to many older people. My parents were only in their late twenties and my grandparents and Granny Emett seemed more modern in comparison. This posse of elderly ladies all seemed to dress in similar dark tones and print frocks with strings of amber beads. I would hear their discreet murmured conversations and feel glad that I lived next door with Granny and Vi who were altogether more lively.

Halford, so pretty and self-contained, was actually a hot bed of gossip and would I imagine have proved fertile ground for Agatha Christie's Miss Marple. In 1939 in those early days of the war, the little village dozing in the sun on the ancient Fosse Way seemed to have altered little from previous times.

Tredington, only two miles away, but on a well-used main road, was very different and where the war became integrated into all our daily lives.

Afternoon tea at Miss Sutton's 'Thatchcot' 1939

Tredington

Tredington, situated on the busy A34 which ran between Birmingham and Oxford, saw RAF and Army lorries rumbling through as the war gathered momentum.

Our new home, The Firs, was a bleak looking bungalow standing in a large bare garden just outside the centre of the pretty village, bounded on one side by the village allotments. Here ugly blackout curtains had to be put up at every window and here food rationing began to take more effect.

Over time, thanks to the non-stop efforts of Granny and Grandpa, the bungalow became a very pleasant, comfortable home set in immaculate lawns and flowerbeds with a large well ordered vegetable garden.

From the first Granny and Grandpa provided a secure and welcoming home where I was very happy to be seeing so much of my parents again.

My father, whose job was still in Birmingham, came down every weekend. My mother lived at 'The Firs' with her parents and with me. After some months my mother took a secretarial job at a firm called Coventry Climax which, due to the war, had re-located to a large house in the village of Newbold not far away.

I remember seeing my mother cycling off to Newbold and could see how glad she was to be returning to the stimulating world of work. She was gregarious and competent and I found out in much later conversations with her that she had missed the fun she always generated during her secretarial jobs before her marriage.

Arriving at the bungalow Grandpa had been surprised to see a very large tarpaulin covering a bulky shape on the main unkempt lawn. On investigation it proved to be a small Austin 7 car. Uncle Ralph had it restored to full working order and the result was that Grandpa was soon pootling about the nearby villages in this tiny car. In the first world war he had been in an early version of the Fleet Airarm and had a lifelong interest in boats and shipping. He now drove as if he was steering a small boat with his head and shoulder out over the passenger door, with his other arm gripping the steering wheel. He also had his pipe firmly clenched between his teeth. Occasionally I accompanied him and lurked in the back feeling rather embarrassed at this method of progress. After some time petrol rationing was enforced and the little car was seen no more.

My father still managed to get enough petrol to drive down to us for the weekends. I longed to see him each weekend and looked out eagerly for his arrival. He came by a circuitous route to avoid passing the policeman's modern house at the Halford and Tredington crossroads. Grandpa would have the bungalow's garage door open and shut it smartly as soon as my father drove in. If the policeman saw him later in the village he must have known that he had driven down, but as there was no sign of the car obligingly turned a blind eye to this activity. Petrol for private motorists was now in short supply.

A nice surprise for us all was the comfort of bath times at the bungalow. The old fashioned bath was situated at one end of the long narrow kitchen, beside the stove which was usually lit and emanating a cosy warmth. In the days before central heating in bathrooms this was a luxury, so that bath times became a particular treat. Unfortunately, during those first months, the bungalow was home to some very large house spiders. Once, when one dropped off the ceiling into my bath and appeared to be swimming towards me, my mother was amazed to see me levitate out of the bath without touching the sides. Such was my horror of big spiders. I vividly remember this event.

To obtain cold water at the kitchen sink an old fashioned hand pump had to be used before water would run from the tap. Dashing in from play I would pump eagerly to get a brimming mug of delicious cold water and would then often carry on pumping to build up a supply of water for Granny to use later.

It was decided that I should go to Tredington village school. Inside the school was one large room divided by a big wooden screen. The headmaster taught the older children and a woman teacher took the rest of us. My memories of what we did are rather hazy. I do remember being rather startled to be given a slate and chalk to work with and then being shown how to knit dishcloths with soft white string and big wooden knitting needles. One memory is of watching a school concert shortly after my arrival.

As my mother had her 'war-effort' job and my father only came at weekends, I saw a great deal of my grandparents.

I loved my Grandpa. Cheerful, hard-working and active, he was a man of few words. Those words were always succinct. He had complete contempt for lies or underhand behaviour but was otherwise kindly and tolerant, if a bit brusque.

Not long after arriving at Tredington he became involved in various voluntary tasks. He visited the village 'hut' daily, keeping it swept and tidy, and dealt briskly with the vagaries of the boiler. This 'hut' was of great importance in the war time village. It was a very large black wooden shed up some steps near the pub, the White Lion. Here were held whist drives, meetings, occasional film shows, social events and dances for the servicemen.

Grandpa also cycled round the nearby villages collecting War Savings, and later raised a large sum of money for the restoration of the church bells. He served on numerous committees. He made very little of this at the time and, as a child, I was almost unaware of these activities, thinking of Grandpa as a permanent fixture in the large garden which he gradually transformed.

When we all first arrived at the bungalow, various village men visiting their allotments would look over the fence at Grandpa's garden. At first with a certain scorn, as Grandpa was not a countryman. As he set about his work in the large vegetable garden digging, raking, seed sowing and watering and tending his crops their scorn turned gradually to admiration.

The garden was large; two lawns, a big vegetable garden, flower beds, fruit bushes, fruit trees an area of rough grass and a spinney. Grandpa worked in the garden every day and kept the property immaculate.

After some time conversations and pipe smoking took place over the fence. Grandpa had a particular crony referred to as 'old Thorn.' He invited Grandpa to have a share in rearing a pig, one of several kept on the allotments. We put out a basket of vegetable peelings, egg shells and so on at the allotment fence several times a week. This was emptied to contribute to pig swill to feed the pigs. In due course Granny was presented with a large salted haunch of bacon which eked out our wartime rations. People were encouraged to form pig clubs so that the animals were fed on household scraps rather than expensive animal feed.

While Grandpa's sphere was mainly outside, either outside in the garden, or outside in the village, Granny by contrast was very domestic and her sphere was definitely the home. She was lovely. Short, pretty and dumpy she always reminded me of Mrs Tiggy Winkle in Beatrix Potter's books, or perhaps of Peter Rabbit's mother. She was gentle and kind but quite merry. Where Grandpa seemed to be forever gardening, Granny seemed to be forever cooking and providing meals for us all.

On Fridays, however, Granny had her weekly morning out. During the school holidays I went with her. We would go on the bus to Stratford, a lovely journey still almost unchanged after all these years. Once alighted from the bus there was a particular routine to follow. First to a newsagent at the bottom of Bridge Street where Granny paid the paper bill and bought me Sunny Stories, a small square comic style paper book for children. I was a very quick reader, reading being my passion. I had learnt to read aged 4½ in my pre-school class in Hall Green, so that by the time we had visited a few more shops I had read Sunny Stories from cover to cover, but happily kept if for re-reading later. After a visit to a very smart grocers we went to Boots to change Grandpa's library book. To help us in this choice Grandpa made a minute pencil dot to the right side of the author's name on the title page. If there was not a dot, it was safe to assume Grandpa had not yet read it.. Sometimes there was a visit to Fred Winters, a smart drapers shop, then finally, Granny's treat. We went together to the Hathaway tea rooms. Here we would greet the ladies behind the counter and then go upstairs to select a pleasant table, by the fire, if it was a cold day. The Hathaway was usually fairly full, being very popular and mainly inhabited by ladies enjoying these superior tea rooms. Occasionally actors from the Shakespeare Memorial theatre were present. They didn't particularly interest me then, although as I grew older their attractions increased.

A waitress would take our order and then bring a large tray with a wide range of delectable buns and cakes displayed. On making your choice it was transferred to your plate by the waitress using tongs.

25

My mother and Granny had long been addicted to tea shops and I remember visits to Barrows in pre-war Birmingham. For the duration of the war, however, the Hathaway was our favourite. These tea rooms were presided over by a large important lady with a shelf like bosom and a commanding manner. She generally stood behind the counter downstairs. On our way out we would stop at this counter and Granny's regular 'Polish cake', reserved for special customers, was brought out, paid for and handed over. This cake was mysterious and special. Its texture was that of a Madeira cake and embedded in each slice were glace cherries and quite large pieces of hard chocolate. These chocolate pieces were in irregular chunks and it puzzled me that they did not melt during the cooking process. This special cake was not large and was saved for Sunday tea where it was much enjoyed.

In general our food at the bungalow was plain and simple, for example slices of Spam and mashed potatoes and perhaps boiled rice with jam, Grandpa's favourite. Grandpa supplied continual fruit and vegetables from the productive garden and Granny spent a good deal of time bottling fruit and salting runner beans for preservation. Nearly every meal seemed to finish with fruit and custard. Sunday lunches were different, delicious meat, vegetables and gravy which were my favourite.

One afternoon a week Granny joined a group of ladies who met at the vicarage to knit for the sailors. This was my first encounter with a country rectory. The house was large, grey, plain fronted and old. In the shabby but comfortable living room village ladies of all shapes and sizes, would knit balaclava helmets and socks in strong oiled navy wool, conversing politely and taking tea. Mrs Stredder, the vicar's wife, was tall and grey haired and gentle. She was kind to me. I was the only child present, so she provided me with a large box of old comics which I avidly perused. Sometimes if it was warm I would wander around their large garden. Here I saw trimmed box hedges for the first time and smelt the distinctive fresh smell of their leaves. Here I first climbed a yew tree – the powdery bark left greenish black stains on my frock.

Tredington Church

The Stredders had a grown-up daughter called Christine, who I think had left home by then. Once Mrs Stredder took me upstairs to Christine's old bedroom where there was a large collection of tiny china animals on her mantelpiece. I was left to look at them or play with them and to look at Christine's books. I remember standing in that lonely bedroom, hearing the gentle murmur of the ladies voices downstairs. As I put back one of the tiny ornaments on the crowded shelf I dropped it onto the tiled fireplace surround below. I was very upset. Miserably I went downstairs and stood by Mrs Stredder's chair and whispered to her that I was very sorry that I had dropped one of Christine's china animals and broken it. Mrs Stredder was very kind and reassuring and made no fuss. She was a lovely lady and popular in the village.

I remember her husband less well as I only really saw him in church. He was short and broad and elderly and sometimes dozed off in part of the service. I think Grandpa knew him fairly well as they were both involved in organising various village events.

I was impressed by the church. It was not small and comfortable like Halford Church, but much bigger and rather empty and gaunt inside. There was a strange elegant old fashioned bier for moving coffins which I found a bit sinister. Granny was on the 'flower rota', so in the holidays I went with her. She had to fill two large brass vases near the altar. Grandpa grew tall 'golden rod' in the flower borders and this often made a good background for whatever other flowers were used. Granny and I went into the vestry for Granny to change the old flowers, renew the water and trim the new ones. Various church vestments were hanging up in there and a very large ancient wooden chest with three locks. I used to wonder what was inside. Quite a few years later, after the war was over, this chest was opened for the first time in many years and the priceless 17 century silver chalices found inside were sold to cover the huge cost of renewing the church roof. A useful miracle. I remember a splendid harvest festival there with window ledges crowded with local produce and special golden loaves baked in the shape of sheaves of corn.

On Saturday afternoons Granny and I used to walk the two miles to Shipston on Stour to visit a small cinema. On looking back I suppose this was so that my parents, who had been living apart during the week, could have some time together.

At the cinema, which was a large concrete shed up a few steps, we queued to get in along with the rest of the Saturday afternoon audience which seemed to consist of numerous small boys with large bottles of Tizer and a few older girls. Sometimes the film broke down and the boys would shout and jeer and throw things at the screen and an irate man would come out to threaten them. Granny and I always sat in the back row in relative calm. After the excitements of the 'pictures' we would be glad to visit Nasons, a cafe, in the Square where they sold large hard rock buns, saffron buns of brilliant yellow and scalding cups of tea. Boarding the bus just outside the cafe we would trundle home contentedly in the twilight both having enjoyed our excursion.

The first Christmas at Tredington was a happy family time. I was allowed to choose from one of the many small fir trees growing in the garden. Grandpa dug it up, put it firmly in a smart brass pot and it was placed on a trolley in the living room. Here it was made over to me to decorate. Mrs Russell, a lady from the village who helped Granny with the cleaning, generously offered her Christmas tree decorations to borrow. Her daughters were grown up and no longer used them. This was a good start as I tied on glass globes of different shapes sizes and colours. I then sprinkled the tree with 'snow', actually irregular lumps of cotton wool and tied on innumerable small home-made decorations and presents. I should think the result was pretty cluttered, but I loved it. My tall father helped fix paper chains from the living room ceiling and we found some holly and mistletoe to finish.

A few days before Christmas I had gone with Grandpa to collect the Christmas turkey. We walked part way to Halford to Rainbows farm where we collected the plucked turkey which Grandpa carried home in a straw bag. How Granny transformed this ugly raw looking purplish white bird into a delicious golden turkey on Christmas Day was a mystery to me. We had Christmas pudding and crackers. Granny also got out her big cut glass bowl to make a delicious fruit salad of tinned pears and strawberries – a concoction she had enjoyed made with fresh fruit in France before the war. We listened to the Kings speech, played games and cards and had a lovely day. Some time over the Christmas break my Uncle Eric, my mother's younger brother, came down with presents for us all.

Sometimes my mother and father and I would walk over to Halford to visit Granny Emett, enjoying this walk through the different seasons. We admired the skilled work of the men who did 'hedging and ditching' and liked seeing early Spring lambs playing together in the fields. It was a quiet walk with almost no traffic. Occasionally we would encounter a very old gentleman cycling in a stately manner on his 'sit up and beg' bicycle. He always had garden produce in his bicycle basket. Once my father pulled me on a sledge after a satisfying snow fall.

Here at Tredington I could enjoy long bouts of reading. Grandpa had a full set of the works of Charles Dickens bound in dark blue leather with tooled embossed covers. They were large, heavy and flat, the pages being almost square rather than rectangular. David Copperfield was my favourite and read from cover to cover.   Each book had many detailed engravings to pore over.   Through these superb illustrations I became familiar with all Dickens astonishing characters and returned again and again to these well-loved volumes. There was also a small plain book with small print and no illustrations. Wind in the Willows by Kenneth Graeme. The magic of this book ignited my imagination and made a very strong lasting impression. To my delight my father also bought me several classic children's books, illustrated with good water colour pictures and bold line drawings: Gulliver's Travels, Alice in Wonderland and Robinson Crusoe. These all-absorbing tales opened up new worlds of interest and excitement.

Once arriving at the dining table before lunch and finding me there engrossed in a book Grandpa said 'No reading at the table'. I immediately put my book away. Several days later I arrived at the table to find Grandpa reading the newspaper, I tweaked it saying 'No reading at the table Grandpa'. My mother and grandmother held their breath. Grandpa, however, always given to fair judgements, laughed rather wryly but put down the paper.

In the evenings, after supper and when Grandpa had as usual done all the washing up, we would all sit round the fire in the living room. My grandparents always sat in pretty old fashioned tub chairs they had preserved all their married life, my mother or both my parents in more modern chairs. I sat on the sofa. We would read, chat and listen to the radio. Granny would often do mending and sewing. Favourite radio programmes were Monday Night at Eight and Tommy Handley in ITMA. When the mellifluous tones of John Snagge or other well-known news readers gave us the war time news these announcements were quite often interpreted for us by Grandpa who could always see to the nub of the matter behind these bracing pronouncements.

I never saw Grandpa worried by the news until the time of Dunkirk when he became unusually subdued for a while.   He was usually a source of cheerful common sense which gave the household its secure foundation.

In the Spring a full size maypole was erected in the school playground and we were taught simple patterns to weave with coloured ribbons as we danced round it thoroughly enjoying ourselves.

By now I had picked up a habit common to my new school friends. If surprised I would say COO ... ER loudly and then clamp my upper teeth over my lower lip. This didn't go down too well at home, and as I didn't seem to be learning very much a decision was made to send me later on to a small boarding school at Stratford on Avon. There I would be a weekly boarder, coming home at the weekends.

This decision was helped forward by the fact that another Tredington girl of my age, Jennifer Guthrie, was already a weekly board at the Croft School in Stratford. Jennifer lived at Tredington Manor. Her father was Captain Guthrie known to Grandpa as they worked together on a village committee, so perhaps Grandpa had been enquiring about schools in the district.

In the meantime my cousin Norma came to stay for a week. Norma was a year younger than I was and we had grown up spending a good deal of time together. She was even tempered and sunny and we played happily together.

We had always been intrigued by visits to small local post offices and had a passion for playing 'Post Offices'. We converted two kitchen chairs into our post office counters where we issued stamps, rubber stamped our pretend documents and were generally officious. Sometimes we played at being office secretaries.

One day we came up with a different plan. We would go into the village together with collecting trays and tins for money. We improvised trays from cardboard box lids suspended from our necks with string and containing some home-made card bound badges. As we set off for the small garden gate we were intercepted by Grandpa, who smiled and asked where we

were off to. 'To the village to collect some money' we told him. 'And what are you collecting for' asked Grandpa. 'For us' we said. We were most disappointed to be told we were not allowed to do this. Money had to be collected for good causes or charities and not for children to spend on themselves. Grandpa was kind but firm. So that was that. We returned to another favourite game of ours, playing Indians with our home made wigwams on the lawn.

Gradually, as time passed, I began to feel stirrings of apprehension at the thought of boarding school looming ever nearer. In some ways I longed to see what it was like but I sometimes felt dismayed. What would it really be like? Only time would tell.

The Croft School, Stratford on Avon

Boarding School

Jennifer and I had become friends by now and sometimes played together. She came to The Firs and I went to the manor. Not having mixed before with any children from an upper class background, I was at first surprised to find that she did not see much of her parents, but was looked after by a nanny. She had an older brother at boarding school and a younger brother at home. When once we did come across her father, a handsome irritable man of florid appearance, it seemed to me that he spoke to her in a tone rather less amicable than that which he used to his dogs.

None of this seemed to affect Jennifer, a healthy attractive girl, self-confident and tough. She told me about the school where I would soon be joining her.

As I was a new girl, starting part way through the school year at the beginning of the Summer Term, it had been suggested that I join the other pupils a day or so after term began. We were offered an afternoon appointment to meet the headmistress.

My mother was very busy now with her job which somehow seemed to be part of the War Effort, so my granny took me, together with my neatly packed suitcase, on the bus.

The school was housed in a large handsome old house looking down Church Street and was altogether more impressive in appearance than my previous three schools. We were ushered into the headmistress's sitting room which was comfortably furnished with Persian carpets and antique furniture despite the rather spartan appearance of the rest of the school.

The moment I set eyes on Miss Phillips I felt my heart sink. She was small, neat and upright with shiny red cheeks and with an air of contained menace. After some general conversation with us both, a few honeyed words indicated to my grandmother that it was time for her to leave. As my darling kind granny bent to kiss me goodbye I turned away, unwilling to show any kind of weakness in front of this new headmistress. I was then taken to join Jennifer and my other classmates.

I managed to cope quite well with the rest of the day but after 'lights out' in the dormitory that night I burrowed right down the bed for some quiet sobbing as I wished that I had kissed Granny goodbye.

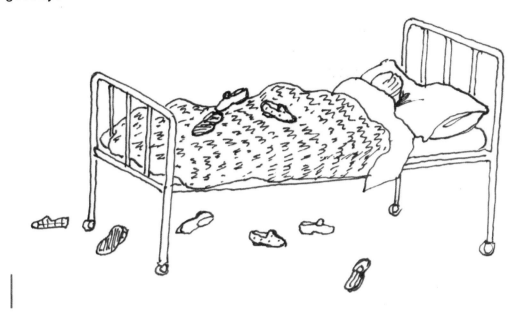

When I woke up next morning I was amazed to find my bed covered in slippers. Apparently I had whimpered in my sleep to such an extent that the other girls had thrown their slippers at my bed in exasperation so that I would be quiet and they could sleep. It must have worked because from then on I slept silently.

From now on I was a weekly boarder at the Croft, coming home to Granny and Grandpa's bungalow every weekend. Jennifer and I travelled backwards and forwards to school on the bus, full of glee every Friday and with resigned gloom on Monday mornings. Some of the older pupils travelling on the same bus kept an eye on us.

There seemed to be so many school rules relating to behaviour and deportment and a large number of prohibitions and practices which I found frustrating after my previous freedom.

For a time on Sunday evenings at the bungalow I would become subdued as bedtime approached. Several times I can remember crying and asking not to go back to boarding school on the Monday morning. My mother would sit on my bed and listen and be kind but implacable. If she had shown any signs of weakening I should have increased the pressure and lengthened my protests. As it was, sensing no change I resigned myself and fell asleep.

Some time later after we had both been in trouble for some kind of petty misdemeanour at school Jennifer and I decided to run away. We were both rebelling over the discipline and restrictions.

We must have realised that our parents might be cross, wanting to return us to school, for we had some vague plan about living in a hay barn and living off apples from a nearby orchard. We must have had very little money, if any, between us, perhaps we were planning to walk all the way home, a feeble plan, even for two eight year olds.

It was summer time with long light evenings. We waited and waited for it to get dark. Eventually we got up and got dressed, intending to get our blazers and outdoor shoes from the downstairs cloakroom near the front door. It was still light, probably about half past nine. We began to creep as quietly as possible down the creaking old wooden staircase.

A teacher intercepted us before we reached the bottom. We were firmly but kindly escorted back to bed. I don't remember any fuss being made. I think Jennifer and I were quite relieved. Responsibility had been taken from us and we could settle down. We were never really sure if anyone realised we had intended to leave the building.

***

In actual fact the school itself was excellent. There were small classes and some good teachers. There were twenty eight boarders ranging from seven to eighteen years old. The head girl named Edwina was I remember both beautiful and kind.

The new lessons were clearly given and easy to follow. It was only later that my problems with mathematics developed. The classrooms in the old house were warm and comfortable. I was surprised and pleased by the amount of time given to games. We had frequent PE lessons each week throughout the year, tennis in summer, hockey in the winter, and netball on our playground. Jennifer also told me there was a Sports Day at the end of the summer.

There was a library where we could borrow books and we had art lessons which I particularly enjoyed.

Apart from the boarders there were also quite a number of day-girls, vaguely despised by the boarders. We felt that because they could go home everyday and did not have to endure the rigours of our after school life they were therefore in some way soft.

After our bread and jam tea we were taken on long walks until supper time by just one teacher. When I became a teacher myself in later years I realised that this rota gave the remaining staff a long pleasant quiet interlude without us. The walks were taken in a neat 'crocodile' walking decorously two by two, headed by two responsible older pupils and brought up at the back by the teacher, each pupil and teacher with their gas mask container over their shoulder.

By the time we got back from our walk we were ravenously hungry. Unfortunately next door to the school was an hotel called The William and Mary from which issued forth delicious smells of sophisticated cooking. In the early days of the war Terry Thomas like types with red sports cars would be seen dashing in and out as we passed in our lagging crocodile. Our supper in contrast would probably be something on toast followed by jam tart and custard, the jam a thin film over the rock hard pastry. A very sharp eye was kept on cost cutting.

On one occasion when I broke a cup and was sent to Miss Phillips to be reprimanded, I remember that she questioned me narrowly. I said truthfully that it came to pieces in my hands as I was washing up. She asked to see the pieces. After an interval these were retrieved from the dustbin. She examined them critically and then said that as both broken edges were stained and not white, there had been a crack in the cup and therefore I would not be charged for the breakage. Grudgingly I conceded to myself that she had been very fair.

The boarders' most hated task was washing up. On a rota system a small team washed up after meals each day. There were always some older pupils to oversee sensible behaviour. The sink was wooden, the washing up water not very hot and the drying cloths soon became sodden. This scullery room was long and narrow with a hatch from the dining room. It always smelt damp. We rarely went inside the big kitchen where meals were prepared by a small staff.

We were taught to make our own beds, very neatly with taut sheets. I rather enjoyed this and still like bed making.

We washed each morning in our dormitories using a jug and basin. In the evenings we washed at basins in the large bathroom. Once a week on a rota system we had a bath there too. Here matron would dole out medicine if necessary. I seem to remember we had a large spoonful of cod liver oil and malt everyday. We were sometimes given a clear pink astringent spoonful of Parrish's Chemical Food which I enjoyed.

With plenty of physical exercise, a fairly meagre diet and a long walk every day most of us were very healthy and lively. A disciplined framework to our day gave us a well-known pattern to follow. Discipline was further maintained by a system of order marks which were tallied each week, the results given to your house prefects. Each pupil was allocated to one of three houses. I was put into St Patrick's, perhaps because of my Irish surname. Every Monday morning playtime there was a house meeting in the playground where the tallied house points were read out by the prefects. Five points were taken away for an 'order' mark, two for a 'neatness' mark. An order mark was only given after clear instructions had been given and if you deliberately failed to comply with the order. They were comparatively rare. A 'neatness' mark was given if you left your possessions where they should not be or if, for instance, you forgot or deliberately flouted the instruction to change from indoor to outdoor shoes for every outdoor play. Your confiscated property was consigned to the lost property box which was actually a large wicker hamper down the steps of a white-washed cellar. You could reclaim your property at the end of the week. Everything you owned or wore had to be clearly marked so retrieval was simple.

After some time it was found that I had lost my house more points than any other pupil. Conforming did not come easily and the many rules and regulations seemed petty. Although I was careless about losing points for myself I did not want to lose points for my house so gradually improved. Although the heads of house were dismayed at my record they just made one strong straightforward complaint and left it at that. There was no pressure or unpleasantness directed at me which is, I think, why I made very real efforts to improve.

There was plenty to explore in this complex new world. The main house of the school was joined to two other old red brick houses to make one long building fronting Old Town.

Our playground backed the main house and had obviously been a large walled garden in pre-school years. Here there was a tall brick wall to play ball games against, a small rather trodden down area, bike sheds, garden beds and an area of shrubbery where we were strictly forbidden to play. Taking up the centre was a netball pitch of gritted earth, if I remember correctly. It certainly wasn't tarmaced. Hopscotch was very popular, leap frog and variations of 'tag' or catch were frequent, and here we gathered to chat with friends, learn new playground rhymes and games and pass on gossip and news.

The dormitories were all upstairs and varied from those housing two beds to ones housing as many as six. There was a small sick room where ill girls could stay until they were better.

We were all encouraged to bring 'tuck' from home which was taken from us and locked away. Every day after lunch the boarders queued up to collect a small amount of their sweets or chocolate which they took into a classroom next to matron's office. Here we sat quietly enjoying our 'tuck' while a teacher read a book to us in serial form, so much every day, before we went out to play in the fresh air. I vividly remember Miss Porter reading 'The Secret Garden' which we found intensely harrowing and exciting. We could hardly wait each day to find out what would happen next. I later borrowed if from the school library to re-read.

I enjoyed being with a group of other very varied children and enjoyed the lessons. Because I was one of the few weekly boarders I also could enjoy the delights and freedom of home. The only reason I went to boarding school was because of the war and looking back I am glad of it. It taught me to be self-reliant from an early age and also taught me that even within a fairly rigid framework individual freedoms could be engineered. My passion was reading and I managed to find extra time to indulge this passion. If I got up very swiftly at the rising bell and washed and dressed with extra speed I could get to the playroom where we assembled before the breakfast gong earlier than the others. Here I could have perhaps a quarter of an hours precious reading. Also, while we spent most of our playground time in a variety of games, we were not prevented from reading if we so wished.

In the playground a luxuriant Chinese Wisteria climbed up and through an elegant narrow wrought iron pergola against the wall of the old house. Near the ground the twisted stems of the wisteria were smooth and thick. Here I found a perfect place to sit and read. I particularly remember enjoying Dr Dolittle books and Girls Crystal comics.

During each term I found we were expected to read several books from a set list in our own time. I found to my delighted surprise that my favourite passion was condoned and encouraged, a real bonus.

***

Something interesting always seemed to be going on at school. As I was an only child without experience of brothers or sisters I was amazed at the continual dramas unrolling before us.

As rows and feuds broke out I was constantly being asked 'Whose side are you on?' Coming from a happy contented home where I had never encountered a row I found this rather mystifying at first, until I learned to be more partisan.

40

About this time I remember the 'chocolate biscuit' incident. Our limited amounts of 'tuck' brought from home were under the control of matron. Apparently one day a parcel containing chocolate biscuits had been sent by a parent and delivered as was usual to matron's office. Halfway through opening the parcel matron had been called away. On her return she found that someone had taken some of the biscuits in her absence. Considering how hungry we usually were I'm surprised there had not been a queue.

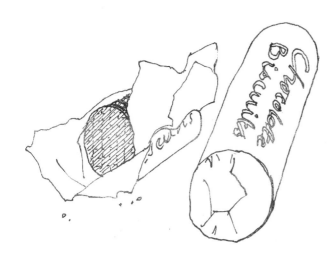

That evening we were all sent for by Miss Phillips. We filed into her sitting room and sat on the floor in neat rows, thankful for the luxurious carpet where we had comfortable ringside seats for the entertainment to come.

Grimly Miss Phillips announced that we had thieves in our midst. We sat up. This sounded promising. Miss Phillips narrated the scenario and then announced in shocked tones that Betty and Dawn had been discovered eating chocolate biscuits only thirty minutes ago, and what had they got to say for themselves.

Betty, short and belligerent, went very red and said nothing. Dopey, willowy Dawn said Betty had given them to her. Betty at first kept silent until under a barrage of threats from Miss Phillips she said truculently that the biscuits were from her lunch time tuck. She had put them in her pocket and then forgotten about them. Half an hour ago she had remembered them and given two to Dawn, eating the rest herself. She sounded so confident that we were all momentarily rather taken aback. Miss Phillips then played her trump card.

'Betty' she said sweetly, 'You all have your tuck at lunch time when you say that you put the biscuits in your pocket, only remembering them a short while ago. Several hours ago all of you changed from your daytime uniform into your after school frocks, so why were the forgotten biscuits not still in your school uniform pocket?'

'Well', muttered Betty 'They must have fallen out of my school uniform pocket into my after school frock pocket without my noticing'.

We all groaned. Even Betty realised she had burned her boats. Disappointed at the quick resolution of the crime we filed out while the culprits remained behind.

Looking back our constant hunger seemed to loom large in a variety of incidents. One in which I was heavily involved was concerned with St Patrick's Day. Once a year on your Saint's day, your entire house was given a day free from lessons. This was keenly looked forward to. One year my particular small dormitory of four girls from my house made a plan. We knew we were to be taken shopping in Stratford during the morning to spend some pocket money. We planned that one of us would surreptitiously buy four really large iced buns and then smuggle them back to school for a midnight feast. We were challenged by the fact that in all the many school stories we read midnight feasts were a frequent feature. Illustrations would show pupils gathered round wicker hampers consuming the goodies within. We were so sharply scrutinised that no hamper would ever make its way into **our** dormitories, but iced buns would be better than nothing.

On the appointed morning we distracted the accompanying teacher while one of us quickly bought the buns, stowing them in their empty gas mask case – the gas mask itself having been hidden back at school. When we got back we had to find a hiding place for them so Enid transferred them to her capacious knitting bag in the classroom cupboard. We were not allowed to go to our dormitories during the day so how were we to smuggle the buns to our room? At bedtime we would be overseen by eagle-eyed matron.

I was having an evening music practice in a small classroom near our bedroom and volunteered to take the knitting bag. As I went noiselessly through the swing door into the dormitory area I looked up and saw Miss Phillips standing at the top of the stairs.

What exactly are you doing Gillian?' was the icy query. 'Just taking Enid's knitting bag to our room Miss Phillips' I said feebly. Miss Phillips didn't even deign to reply and I slunk back. The others were furious that I hadn't managed my mission. That night in bed, bunless and disappointed it was decided we would have to get rid of them. We would have to get to the classroom cupboard where the buns were still reposing and eat them before breakfast. If they were found we would all be in trouble. I volunteered to go first as it was felt I had let the group down.

Next morning washing and dressing with suspicious speed I made my way to the big classroom cupboard, switched on the light and shut the door and began eating. The large bun was delicious although I could have done with a glass of water to help it down. Just as I was finishing, hoping to be replaced by the next conspirator the door opened a crevice to anguished whispering from outside. Apparently the teacher on duty had appeared earlier than usual and wanted to gather the pupils to talk about library books. 'You'll have to eat them all' came a desperate hiss and the door was closed before all the pupils gathered round the teacher.

The second bun was not quite so delicious, the third bun was difficult, the fourth was a nightmare. Without even a sip of water to help down the glutinous mass, and worried by the falsely bright voices of my fellow conspirators just outside the door trying to distract the teacher who eventually wanted to open the cupboard door to collect the class registers, I felt as though I might choke to death.

At length, unnoticed by the teacher I tottered out, pale and sticky. I was cheered by my colleagues praise, but faint at the thought of ploughing my way through breakfast porridge. As I was known to have a keen appetite rejecting my porridge would have meant a visit to the dreaded sick bay and matron's questions. I managed and we survived. No one ever mentioned a midnight feast again.

It took me some time to realise that the lynch-pin of the Croft School teaching staff was probably Miss Porter.

Miss Porter, perhaps in her late thirties, was energetic and full of enthusiasm. She was a born teacher and an organising genius. It was Miss Porter who organised the complex teaching and grading of our deportment marks each week. Miss Porter who organised and directed our yearly Sports Day. Miss Porter who devised the school drama productions, putting on plays with acting, costumes and scenery of a high standard.

Miss Porter taught most school subjects except maths and French - I was abysmal at both. In all other subjects I did well entirely because of her excellent teaching.

I suppose the best way to describe her would be to say that she was bracing. She expected and got a high standard of work from all her pupils. She divided up all learning activities, in hockey, tennis, PE, Geography, English, Art and so on into small easy steps with very careful progression so that her pupils found learning easy in her subjects. We thought her a bit fierce but respected her sterling qualities. She was also quick witted and brave. These qualities she showed to perfection in the drowning boy incident.

Because our school was situated in the town itself, we had to walk some distance to the recreation grounds opposite the theatre to play hockey or practice sports. Part of the journey involved crossing the river in a flat bottomed 'chain' ferry boat. One day, after games, we were lined up waiting for the ferry to return across the river for us when a small boy standing too near the river bank fell in. The sides were steep.

The Stratford Chain Ferry

Immediately Miss Porter lay on the bank, told us crisply to sit on her to anchor her while she leant out over the water. As the curled up pale boy rose dimly to the surface for the third time she grabbed him firmly and pulled him out – no easy task, as he was about six or seven years old and his clothing was completely sodden. He stood shivering violently with water pouring from his mouth, ears, eyes and nose. Miss Porter made his dazed older sisters support him and rush him home.Our admiration knew no bounds. We felt that we would always be safe with Miss Porter around.

Under Miss Porter's coaching I learned hockey and tennis and enjoyed acting in the plays she directed. In her art lessons she taught us how to make clear accurate drawings. At the age of eight we learned how to draw in perspective and how to draw a perfect ellipse. Every attempt was patiently and firmly appraised, corrected and improved. At the time I was not really aware of her enormous influence but only knew that when she was about we tended to be well behaved and happy. On one occasion, during a recreation period, I remember her playing the piano for us to gather round to sing popular wartime songs. She was an influence for good in all our lives.

As to the war itself I don't remember that many of us had much idea of what was going on. Some girls had fathers in the armed forces. None of us ever seemed to imagine that we would not win the war eventually. No one seemed frightened.

We heard dramatic stories of Birmingham, and particularly Coventry, being badly bombed but felt removed from these experiences in the country. We saw convoys of lorries constantly passing along main roads. We saw aircraft hangars erected in the fields, large half-circles of corrugated iron painted with camouflage. Occasionally there would be stories of enemy parachutes coming down and local farmers holding Germans at bay until army personnel arrived. Aerodromes were built, Nissan huts erected and concrete pillboxes with gun emplacements were placed at strategic crossroads. There was copious use of barbed wire. We heard that many beaches were now completely blocked off by barbed wire barricades, although no one went on holidays to find out for themselves.

I loved another of Uncle Fred's Punch cartoons about a wired off beach because I so admired the way he had drawn the teetering bus from a low perspective.

"I said, the Englishman's traditional love of the sea is going to have serious consequences if you don't coax a few of them off the top."

All the news, radio shows, newspapers and general publications were upbeat in character. There was a distinct feeling that 'we were all in this together' and a plucky attitude was required and admired. Looking back I can see that this was a deliberate form of propaganda. However a genuine camaraderie and feeling of determination was to be experienced by many. Most of us were not aware of the cynical profiteering that accompanies most wars – it simply did not come within our experience.

I was aware that occasionally the entire village of Tredington would be sadly subdued by learning of the terrible grief some families had to endure as all their precious children were killed in action. At the Croft we were all involved in the scheme for National Savings and bought stamps weekly to support the War Effort. We all knew that we were very lucky compared to so many.

Pre-war memories began to feel very distant by this time. I no longer dreaded going back to boarding school every Monday. School with all its activities and friends and new experiences was good, especially as I was still able to come back to my family at The Firs every weekend.

Tredington Holidays

Tredington Holidays

During the summer holiday I was given a baby wild rabbit. Its mother had been shot and the babies were offered round the village. Grandpa carried one home for me and quickly knocked together a rough and ready rabbit hutch. The rabbit was soft and pretty and happy to be picked up gently and stroked. As it was so young we gave it wheat germ mixed into milk and

a saucer of water to drink. Later it liked lettuce and dandelion leaves too. As weeks passed and it grew bigger it became restless. It began to gnaw at the base of the hutch's wooden door. We realised it would be cruel to keep it. After all it was a wild rabbit not a tame domestic one.

In the spinney that was part of the bungalow's grounds there were several rabbit holes at the base of the trees. Grandpa helped me carry the hutch down there before going back to his gardening.

I sat beside the hutch and opened the door. After some time the rabbit came out and hopped about before disappearing down one of the rabbit holes. I waited quietly. Ten minutes later to my surprise the rabbit came back and went into the hutch. We returned to the bungalow garden. A day or two later I repeated the experiment. This time the rabbit went quickly down the rabbit hole and didn't come back. I was sad, but at the same time pleased because we had protected it until it was old enough and strong enough to fend for itself. Once it became unhappy I did not want to keep it a prisoner.

The small spinney contained dark conifers and bushes on the banks of a stream which marked the boundary of grandpa's land. This stream went under a small bridge to pass under the road and join the river Stour on the opposite side of the road. I'm sure it was because of these conifers and their thick cover that I saw two interesting birds that Summer.

Looking out of the kitchen window one afternoon we saw to our astonishment a very large owl perched in a spindly tree on the rough grass area which was backed by the spinney. The owl looked dazed and acutely embarrassed. It was being mobbed by a gang of small birds who seemed outraged at finding it about in daylight. We thought perhaps it usually roosted in the cover of the spinney. Eventually it flapped back there with the angry small birds still in noisy pursuit.

Some days later I heard high pitched squeaking and screeching sounds as a little flock of tiny birds swooped and darted about over the grassland. One perched on a twig long enough for me to see a little bright orange streak of feathers on the top of its head, and its dark wing barred with white. My bird book identified it as a gold crest, one of Europe's smallest birds. Further reading informed me that it made a cup shaped nest of moss and spiders webs suspended from a branch of a conifer tree.

So within the space of a few days I had seen both the largest and smallest wild birds I had encountered so far.

Aunty Vi had identified many wild flowers and trees for Jean and I at Halford and now Norma and I had begun to take an interest in birds, so this double sighting was very satisfactory.

About this time I began collecting birds eggs, quite a common activity in those days, although now I am not happy I did this.

It happened because sometimes in my wandering about the village I visited Mr and Mrs Aspinall who lived up a steep grassy slope on the other side of the spinney stream. Mr and Mrs Aspinall kept hens and provided eggs for people in the village. Mr Aspinall looked a bit like George Bernard Shaw, only with brown clothes and a brown beard. Mrs Aspinall used to sometimes ask me in, give me lemonade to drink and let me play the game of solitaire with a board full of bright glass marbles.

On one visit they showed me wild birds' nests in their boundary hedge and showed me how to collect their eggs. They told me that you must never startle or upset the mother bird

sitting on her nest whose eye would regard you steadfastly. Only if she flew off for a while could you quickly and gently remove just one egg. Later they showed me how to pierce a small hole in one end of the egg with a pin and then make a slightly larger hole at the other end. You then blow gently into the small hole and the liquid contents of the egg come out of the larger hole. You had to do this carefully, noticing the direction of any breeze so as to avoid getting egg yolk on your clothes. You were left with a delicate fragile 'blown' egg shell with the exquisite colours of the different bird's eggs. I particularly liked the blue and turquoise ones.

School children often collected birds eggs and natural history museums had drawers full of beautiful specimens to admire. I am surprised now that I did such a thing and realise how much attitudes have changed to such activities.

I enjoyed exploring the bungalow's large garden. I loved the peppery smell of a large bed of lupins in the hot sun and admired the deep pink japonica flowers under the bedroom window. None of us liked the profusion of marigolds that had been planted by the bungalow's previous owners all around the front door but I can't think why. Soft pink roses grew on a trellis down to the small front gate. There was a much larger wider gate to the garage entrance and I enjoyed swinging on this, watching convoys of RAF and Army lorries driving by. Sometimes the soldiers and airmen waved to me.

My father rigged up clock golf on the large lawn and we played together at weekends. I particularly enjoyed this game because I found that I had a good eye for distances. My mother and I would play ball on the smaller lawn in the Summer evenings

Every day Grandpa spend some time cutting up pieces of wood into logs for the fire and I would go to find him and to chat. Once he laid a long plank over the sawing horse so that Jennifer and I could use it as a see-saw. I would pick fruit for Granny, gooseberries, Victoria plums and raspberries. Sometimes I would eat an apple while it was still on the tree, taking bites out of it while it was still attached to the tree by its stalk just leaving the apple core hanging there. This seemed fun but I stopped doing this after a while thinking it was a bit babyish.

With hindsight I realise how generous and warm was the welcome given to us by my grandparents. My parents felt carefree at the bungalow and they knew I was happy there. Any fears about the outcome of the war were kept from me.

My mother was devoted to her mother. They used to retreat to Granny's bedroom to have chats. Once in passing the open door I heard Granny say to my mother, 'I can't think where I have put that child's present.' This was a week or so before my birthday. 'Oh I know Granny' I called 'it's in your wardrobe at the bottom behind your shoes.' I think I was rather a trial to Granny. It must have been difficult for her to share what would have been a peaceful retirement with an inquisitive and determined grandchild. One mollifying circumstance was that my mother had been even worse so in a sense Granny was used to this kind of behaviour.

Once when Norma was staying with us, I incited her to join with me in making a cardboard sign saying 'Maud the nagger' which we hooked over the bow on the back of Granny's apron which she then wore for several hours. I feel ashamed of this now, because I loved my Granny dearly. Once after my hair had been washed I had neglected to comb or brush it so that it dried in tangles. Very patiently Granny sat down and gently combed my hair until all the tangles were smooth.

Where Granny was always kind and comforting Grandpa was stimulating, a happy combination as far as I was concerned.

Children were always being given sweets in those days and if ever I had any I'd find Grandpa in the garden to offer him one. He would rummage about in the paper bag and take two or three. Sometimes in the evening he gave me blocks of hard toffee marked off into squares. A little hammer was needed to break them up.

All this sweet eating, common in those days, was very bad for my teeth and resulted in some dreaded visits to the dentist in Sheep Street in Stratford. The dentist was American, so one good thing about visiting his dental surgery was the large collection of colourful American comics and magazines in the waiting room.

When it was my turn I had to endure some painful drilling of my teeth. It was also noticed that my teeth were growing crookedly in my mouth so I had two out and then had to wear a

dental plate to encourage the remaining teeth to re-align themselves more neatly. I remember the horrible feeling as warm wax was pressed to the roof of my mouth to make an impression for the dental plate which would hold an adjustable wire against my top teeth. All this was worthwhile however as, after some time, the plate was discarded and my teeth developed evenly, a big improvement.

All these dental visits were made bearable by the quiet, encouraging dentist. He was well respected in the town.

Once Jennifer's older brother David, home for the holidays, took us for a short adventure on a raft he had made to float on the river near the manor under a tunnel of dark trees. The river was so shallow in places that we didn't travel very far although we set off with high hopes.

Jennifer and I found a place to enjoy the river opposite the bungalow. Slipping through the iron railing we went down the bank. The steep river bank opposite was poached with hoof prints where the cattle in the field came down to drink. To the right, where the spinney stream joined the main river was a whirlpool. We kept well away. To the left we found a short stretch of river where we could see the river bed beneath the silvery water. Green clumps of weeds like hair were soft and cushiony. Here the water was too shallow for pretend swimming but just right to cool off on a hot summer's afternoon.

Grandpa loved company and always welcomed visitors. Friends from Birmingham came and Norma and her parents. Eric, my mother's younger brother came once on his powerful motor bike. My father took me for a ride on it as I rode pillion, my arms around his waist, there being no crash helmets or health and safety rules in those days.

Once Jean came for a visit. I was so happy to see her. Eagerly I instructed her in the making of home-made bows and arrows, my current craze. I was used to doing this but it was unfamiliar to Jean. When she cut her thumb quite deeply with our sharp knife I was horrified. I rushed her to my mother who sat her down in the kitchen to have her cut cleaned and bandaged. Jean was very brave and didn't blame me although it was clearly my fault for being thoughtless. My mother asked me to hold her bandaged hand gently while she selected a neat safety pin to secure it. Feeling the throbbing of Jean's thumb beneath the white bandage I felt sick and faint, although Jean kept calm. She was a lovely friend.

I had plenty of occupations of my own, especially for when it was too cold or wet to play outside. I liked drawing and colouring, and making intricate butterflies from Glitterwax. This was a stiffish modelling material in different colours. When warmed gently on a little ledge by the fireplace it became soft enough to model and then cooled to a shiny brittle finish.

I had a small collection of miniature farm animals, jig-saws, a doll and a favourite little painted wooden horse. In the garden there was a swing and a wall to practice hand stands against. In autumn the tall holm oaks, in the hawthorn hedge that fronted onto the road, let down literally thousands of large creamy acorns, some of which I collected to play with.

As a family we would play bagatelle, dominoes and different card games, particularly Happy Families. Grandpa loved cards and went to regular whist drives at the village hut. My mother and I often played 'I-spy' together. She was always good natured and even tempered. I often asked her to tell me about when she was little and apparently naughty and wilful. I loved these tales and liked to hear them over again. Perhaps because she had been so naughty and headstrong she seemed very understanding and not critical. She was loving and kind, but firm and sensible too. Having had a happy childhood she was able to create one for me.

My mother and father were very happy together and always enjoyed each others company. I took this completely for granted and was surprised later to find this happy relationship did not always exist between the parents of some of my friends.

My father and I were alike in our interests and attitudes in many ways. He came from an 'arty' family. His grandfather had been a court lithographer. One of his cousins was a successful artist in Fleet Street and now his brother was an increasingly famous cartoonist. He seemed to know what I needed almost before I did myself.

One Saturday when he arrived at The Firs he carried a large heavy cardboard box. After lunch he told me it was a present for me. I went into the living room to examine the present. He had managed to get hold of a second hand set of Arthur Mee's Encyclopaedias for Children. These big encyclopaedias, bound in dark blue, became an instant source of pleasure, both then and for years to come. Before the days of television or the internet they opened up the world for me being such a rich depository of information with copious illustrations, both black and white and in full colour.

53

First I rushed through all the stories and legends from many lands. Then my interest was taken by the story of art, art history in all its richness with continual surprises and interest. Here I saw all the great masterpieces of the world. Here I saw Michelangelo's 'David' for the first time looking at the superlative sculpture with awe and wonder. Then Geography, History, Natural History and Science all revealed their complexity. Because these books were written for children the information was easy to assimilate.

I pored over the coloured illustrations of moths, butterflies and caterpillars from around the world, hardly able to believe that such fantastic creatures could exist.

This present was typical of my father. Not only was this treasure house of knowledge such fun to investigate, but it proved of invaluable help throughout my schooldays.

One aspect of these books was I suppose less than ideal. The encyclopaedia had been put together from many issues of Arthur Mee's papers for children which had come out over a long period in serial form. As much of the material had been assembled when the British Empire still proudly held sway, there was a 'jingoistic' and overly-patriotic flavour to its attitude at times. In the eyes of the writers, Great Britain was certainly seen as the centre of the world and of great importance. This was rather enjoyable for me at the time but later I began to find some of the views over simplistic and patronising, but overall this did little to detract from the usefulness of these books.

My father and I sometimes had outings of our own. Before the war he and his brother had used a little green and white boat in the river at the bottom of Granny Emett's field. Now, in it, my father rowed me along the stretch of river beside the field towards Halford Bridge. I particularly remember the ripples of light on the underside of the arch of the old stone bridge as we went underneath.

Another time we cycled out one Sunday morning to where the road overlooked a prisoner of war camp for Italians near Ettington Park. Behind a tall wire fence we could see what looked like a relaxed and amicable world. Men were queuing up in the sunshine to have their hair trimmed by an obviously experienced Italian barber and it looked and sounded volatile and jolly, although perhaps we just caught them on a particularly pleasant sunny morning. They wore bright blue outfits with a large orange circle on the front.

I remember the Christmas we all walked over to Thatchcot on Boxing Day, having been invited to tea by Miss Sutton. We had been gently instructed by Aunty May not to arrive before four o'clock as Miss Sutton's afternoon rest was sacrosanct. We enjoyed the two mile walk beside the wintry hedges, then down to Halford Bridge, up the other side and so to Thatchcot. It was very unusual for Granny and Grandpa, my parents and I all to be on a joint outing on foot. I felt an excited anticipation of the delights to come. We arrived as the church clock was striking four to be welcomed into the warm cottage by Aunt May.

The proceedings began with an impressive tea. Miss Sutton presided at the head of the table. The main feature was a superb Dundee cake made by Miss Sutton. Grandpa, who had been accorded a place at Miss Suttons right hand, was a great admirer of this cake. While the adults talked and we had our tea I enjoyed looking round the room. Everything seemed to sparkle. Christmas greenery decked the low beams and there was a small hot intensely glowing fire. Christmas decorations glittered.

After tea we played games. I remember 'Hunt the thimble' which I was often allowed to win. Then Granny Emett and Vi came to join us from their cottage next door. All nine of us sat round the cleared table to play 'Donkey grab'. The aim was, I think from distant memories, to get particular card sequences. You were all dealt a hand of cards, then passed a card to your left hand neighbour before accepting a card from your neighbour on your right, repeating this at a given signal. When you had collected your sequence you put it down in front of you and with lightning speed grabbed a small crab apple from a row set down the centre of the table.

Everyone else then grabbed one and someone was always 'out' as there was one apple short of the number of players. There was a good deal of fun in the game to begin with. After some time however we ran into difficulties which we eventually discovered were caused by the two Grannies.

Granny Emett whose sight was poor had dropped some of her cards onto the floor in her excitement. Granny Goodenough who was so mild and law-abiding was also extremely obstinate in a quiet way. She was very reluctant to pass a card to her left hand neighbour until she had seen the new card arrive from her right, strictly against the rules. There was much good humoured hilarity when these problems had been spotted and set right, so that we could all carry on with the game.

Later, walking home through the frosty dark, we all agreed we had thoroughly enjoyed our Boxing Day visit to Thatchcot.

Arriving at Thatchcot

As time passed I got to know Tredington more thoroughly. Wide grass verges and the village green made the village spacious and attractive.

There was a small general shop and post office presided over by a pleasant, middle aged lady named Mrs Barnes, a fund of useful information according to Grandpa. There was also a small antique shop run by Mrs Jamieson, a tall lady, of independent views, not altogether Grandpa's cup of tea. I liked visiting her because she kept two friendly baby goats in her gated garden.

One pretty house was inhabited by actors and various children, all good looking and rather an exotic addition to the village. Here lived a lady whose stage name was Linda Darnell. She appeared in 'The Ghost Train' a popular film of the time which was one of several that I saw projected onto a screen in the village Hut to an eager audience.

Mr and Mrs Wilkes lived in their handsome substantial farmhouse between the manor and the large churchyard. Mr Wilkes was often to be seen on a glossy horse in the environs of the village.

Down a steep lane beyond the churchyard gate was a tall mill house beside the river. Here lived a fierce old patriarch surrounded by a bevy of deferential elderly daughters.

Sometimes, to my astonishment, my mother would dance with the servicemen at dances for the forces in the Hut. Wives and daughters attended and I remember a good-natured crowd all enjoying themselves.

A very large old barn fronting onto the village green was now designated to be the 'salvage barn'. Everyone brought their saved up newspapers. Here they were neatly bundled to await collection. 'Salvage' was an important concept in the War. To avoid using raw materials we were all urged to collect and re-use whatever we could. Everyone used their gardens and allotments to grow much of their own food and practised home economies of every kind.

There were two tall stalwart men who were fixtures in the village surroundings. One was red-faced 'Warren', the village policeman, usually pushing his bicycle and another was the 'road man' who kept all the village roads, verges and ditches in good order.

Once the road man was clearing a kerb when my mother was walking me with my suitcase up to the White Lion early one Monday morning to put me on the bus to boarding school. 'Well little missy', enquired the kindly road man, 'and how do you like being sent away to school?' This was early on in my time at the Croft and perhaps my steps were reluctant. As I opened my mouth to reply 'She loves it,' intecepted my mother swiftly cutting short my possibly plaintive reply! She was probably right as I grew to enjoy boarding school after my initial reluctance.

Occasionally I would spot the 'knife man' who made his way round the village with his knife grinding machine powered by his busy pedalling. Cottagers would bring out their knives and tools to be sharpened.

All these new people widened my experience, an experience that became very varied. One day I might be playing marbles on the hard packed earth floor of a little terrace cottage where a small boy from the village school lived. The next day I could be walking in dazed delight down a glorious scented herbaceous border in the grounds of the manor. Village people of every kind seemed to live cheek by jowl quite harmoniously. There might have been resentful undercurrents, as some had so little and some so much, but I knew nothing of them. There was no subservience of any kind that I observed and the villagers had a healthy self-respect. Perhaps because my grandfather had become respected in the village I was welcomed everywhere.

One event that seemed to unite all the disparate elements of the village was the yearly church fete.

Grandpa helped to organise the fete and took a big interest in all its ramifications. I went along for the whole afternoon with my mother and grandmother. It was lovely. The fete always seemed to take place in perfect Summer weather in the vicarage grounds. Large marquees were erected for displays of fruit and vegetables and there were competitions for home-made cakes and preserves. The tea hut did a brisk trade. There were stalls, a tombola, a treasure hunt game, bowling for a pig and a greasy pole for the village lads to try their skill.

All the village men were present in snowy shirts with rolled up sleeves showing their sinewy brown forearms. Their wives were rather more shapeless and bashful in their best summer frocks. Children wove ceaselessly in and out. Knowing and laconic remarks were exchanged. I didn't really understand their import but understood the joking was good humoured. Everyone seemed to be enjoying themselves. I encountered the subdued filtered light in the tents and the smell of crushed grass underfoot for the first time. I have enjoyed village fetes ever since.

About this time Uncle Fred illustrated a volume of Walter de la Mare's poems, titled Bells and Grass.   My favourite picture of his illustrated a poem about a mysterious night bird. After that I found more of Walter de la Mare's books and was particularly fascinated by his slightly sinister 'Memoirs of a Midget'. I continued to read at every opportunity.

Our final Christmas at Tredington was particularly cold with snow. I had caught measles, perhaps at school just before the break-up for the Christmas holidays. I was in bed over the holiday period feeling rather wobbly but happy with all the 'visits' from my mother and father and others who came to sit with me. I was quite seriously ill for a while.

The best thing was that instead of sleeping in my usual small bedroom I had a bed in my parents large room at the end of the bungalow. Here, unusually, a proper fire was laid and lit. I loved it when Grandpa came in briskly to tend to the fire on and off throughout the day. To fall asleep in a dark bedroom with snow falling outside and rosy firelight flickering on the walls was very comforting.

The doctor came to visit several times. He was a large tweedy Scotsman with a rich gravelly voice. His air of certainty and kindly authority was reassuring. He reminded my parents that during the day the curtains should be kept drawn against the brilliant light of sun and snow. They complied, but unknown to them I used to pull back the curtain by my bed to read comics and Christmas present books until my eyes were tear-filled and sore. The result of this thoughtless behaviour was that my sight gradually became slightly blurred and by the end of the war I had to wear glasses.

This was the Christmas that Uncle Fred sent me a Christmas card he had made for me. It was of stiff card. On the front elephants, with clothes of stuck on fabrics, were going carol singing. They held a lantern made out of a 'Chinese lantern' seed head, cut in half and stuck down with a tiny bulb inside. This was wired to a minute battery in the hinge of the card. When you opened the card the lantern lit. I was so delighted with this and demonstrated it so often that the battery was used up by the evening of Boxing Day.

Buckley Green Farm, Henley in Arden

When we first moved from Birmingham at the outbreak of the war, no one had any idea of how long it would continue.

As it showed no signs of abating my parents made new plans. They decided on a move for the three of us to live in a flat, which was part of Buckley Green Farm just outside Henley in Arden. Henley was not too far from my father's work or from the Croft School at Stratford.

My Granny Goodenough at the Firs in Tredington was not strong. All the extra shopping, laundry and catering were tiring for her and my mother was also concerned that I was getting a bit of a handful for Granny as I grew older. So we parted on loving terms and with much gratitude and began a new phase in our lives in the Spring of the next year.

I couldn't wait to see the farm and was excited by the prospect of a new life to explore, especially as I knew that we would keep in very close touch with both Grannies and with Grandpa.

The farm was about a mile from Henley which was itself roughly half way between Stratford and Birmingham. A narrow lane led off the A43 over a little bridge and wound half a mile to the farm which was set well back from the road behind a paddock. It was a substantial building, part Tudor and part later additions, and was backed by a semi-circle of hills. A large old red brick barn stood to one side.

Our 'flat' consisted of two light airy rooms high in the apex of the building, chosen to be our living room and my parents' bedroom. At the front the view from the living room was of the paddock and barn below and a field on the far side of the lane. From my parents' back bedroom window we looked down on the trees and bushes round the pond and the lovely circle of hills.

One step down from my parents' room was a long dark loft which contained the farm's big water tank under its steeply pitched roof. Our kitchen was a small part of this loft, under a skylight to let in the daylight. My mother had new shelves, a cupboard, a table, a small portable cooker and a sink in the rather cramped space.

My bedroom was down a narrow flight of stairs to the first floor. It was a large rather dark room with one small window looking out above the front door of the farm. There were metal bars at the window opening as this had been a room for young children previously.

The farm was owned and run by Miss Wenham, a small spare aristocratic woman, deeply tanned and fit. She always wore breeches and a jacket, shirt and tie. I felt a bit wary of her and her clipped way of speaking, although she was pleasant when we met.

We shared a bathroom with Miss Wenham. This was in the old Tudor part of the building above the farm kitchen. It had creaky floors and oak beams. This 'sharing' must have called for delicate negotiations and timing but I was not aware of any of this at the time.

My parents soon made our rooms comfortable. In the living room were our familiar dining table and chairs, our sideboard and bureau and our sofa and chairs all of which must have been brought out of storage. The furniture in our bedrooms also reappeared from our Hall Green days.

Not long after our arrival we acquired a young female cat and named her Minna. She became my close companion. She was one of several cats who lived on the farm. She slept in a farm barn each night and arrived each morning smelling sweetly of hay. She was a tabby cat with markings of black, grey and a warm tawny colour. When I curled up to read on the sofa she would curl up beside me and I could hear and feel the reverberations of her contented purring.

Miss Wenham had a housekeeper who had a small son named Trent. He had red hair and freckles and was a year or two younger than me, perhaps about eight. We became friendly. His mother was a good cook and delighted Miss Wenham with hearty food and steamed jam puddings to fuel her continual activity on the farm.

Miss Wenham was tolerant. As long as Trent and I closed all gates carefully we were free to roam where we would. I found that the farm consisted mainly of cornfields and a hay meadow on the level and pasture for the animals on the fields and hills at the back of the farm. There was a Dutch barn in a large rickyard and a square complex of red brick farm buildings nearby. There was a small orchard, a large pond with resident moorhens and a small triangular field close to the farm, home to particularly beautiful wild flowers. Ducks and hens roamed freely. I seem to remember that the ducks were shut up for the night by Miss Wenham's landgirl and the chickens roosted in the branches of the trees round the pond. The landgirl fed the ducks in the morning and let them out each day.

I don't remember many young men working on the farms. I expect they were in the forces.

The older farm workers wore a kind of uniform – caps on their heads, collarless shirts and waistcoats, old trousers often tied at the knee above their boots. They seemed a tough laconic bunch, never seeming to hurry, but working steadily and tirelessly, a few really old. They were all necessary now as farms were so important, increasing our food yields to feed our country now that so many ships with imported goods could not get through the German blockades.

Because Miss Wenham owned the land we roamed about on, no one seemed cross to see Trent and I there. We soon got used to walking through the farm's herd of dairy cows. I liked their sweet grassy breath and long eye lashes. They were placid and calm. There were several young Clydesdale cart horses usually working on the farm or in the stables. If they were released into the fields we kept away. On summer evenings they would sometimes play, racing up and down the hill and steep field slopes, casting up great clods of earth from their hooves and making the earth tremble beneath them. Once harnessed for work they became calm and reasonable.

There was a large Hereford bull named Bill and we kept away from him too as we were not sure of his temper. Miss Wenham bred prize winning sheep. Before they went off to compete at agricultural shows she washed their fleeces in Persil! Once, coming round the corner of the Dutch barn, I came across her clipping some fleece off the back of a firmly held sheep. As she removed the creamy wool a gaping red wound was revealed, alive with maggots. She briskly got rid of the maggots, dusted the wound with disinfectant powder and released the sheep. I was rather horrified but realised something of the hard reality of rearing animals. It was only because of my roaming around that I had come upon this scene. Neither of us spoke about it and I went on my way feeling a new respect for her.

Trent and I liked to go paddling in the small river. To reach it for part of the way we walked through a cornfield. You had to keep exactly to the path which cut through it diagonally, leading to further fields and the river.

I enjoyed seeing the greenish heads of wheat ripen and turn golden and we sometimes ate the creamy grains when the wheat was ripe.

The lane up to Buckley Green farm continued past our paddock for about a quarter of a mile. Nearly opposite the gate to our paddock was a cottage where Miss Findon lived with her brother. I don't remember ever glimpsing the brother but saw Miss Findon quite often. She regularly went down to Henley in her pony and trap. Continuing past her cottage and the entrance to various fields you came to Mobb's Farm and the end of the lane. Here they bred Hereford bulls which before the war had been exported to the Argentine.

One hot summer's afternoon I was cycling up the lane from Henley when I saw one of these massive bulls being walked towards me by one of Mobb's farm workers. Perhaps he was exercising the bull, or perhaps the bull was being taken to one of the other farms. I moved to the side of the lane as far as I could get into the hedge and stood quiet and still. The farm man nodded to me but did not speak. The bull rolled its eye at me but did not pause in its pacing, placing its hooves lightly on the warm tarmac of the shady lane, its huge weight juddering as its muscles moved beneath its glossy hide.

The man led it by a pole hooked through a ring in the bull's nose. I felt that this magnificent animal was rather embarrassed by this encounter so did not stare. When they had passed by I got back on my bicycle feeling that I had seen something special. I hurried home to tell my mother about it.

I enjoyed cycling up and down the lane. It was narrow and bordered in places with verges creamy with tall cow parsley in the summer. It passed one or two farms. The last farm before the bridge, at a sharp corner was a lovely old half-timbered black and white farm. Here they kept guinea fowl. I liked the sounds they made like the squeaky pumping up of a bike tyre. I sometimes picked up a few of the lovely speckled guinea fowl feathers where they had drifted onto the lane.

Around this time I was given a small tent. At harvest time Trent and I asked if we could sleep out in my tent one night. Neither of us had ever slept out before. We were given permission and made up our groundsheet and blanket beds excitedly. I think we went to bed about half past eight. My parents looked in to check that we were comfortable before they went down the lane for an evening walk. We were getting sleepy by this time.

There was an enormous harvest moon lighting up the sky. Miss Wenham and the farm workers nearby were finishing off the last straw ricks as the harvest was gathered in. The rick yard was just over the hedge from where we had our tent in part of the farm's garden. As the workers' task was eventually completed just before we dropped off to sleep we heard Miss Wenham call crisply to her farm manager, "Thank you John".

John sang out in his country burr "Don't thank me, thank the Lord". This seemed to silence Miss Wenham who usually liked to have the last word. For some reason this struck Trent and I as being very funny and we fell asleep giggling drowsily.

When we woke in the morning we found Hemp the sheepdog lying across the entrance to the tent. Apparently he had lain guarding us all night. A comforting discovery. He usually spent the night sleeping beside Miss Wenham. She had a bed made up permanently outside the back of the farm, sheltered by a tiled roof, but open at the front so that she slept outside in the fresh air for most of the year which surprised and impressed me. Perhaps she had directed the dog to look after us.

65

To help my mother I cycled down into Henley every Saturday morning to collect our small weekly meat ration from Mr Hawkes the butcher in his smart shop.

Henley was a pretty town of half-timbered houses and cottage on either side of its long main street. Close to the centre of this long street, behind the ancient Beaudesert Church was a very steep hill called the Mount where, long before, there had been a castle dominating the settlement below. The buildings in the High Street were very varied. Some were modest terrace cottages, others large handsome houses. There was a steep bike ride up to the station on the other side of the main road where I now caught the train to the Croft School at Stratford each week.

* * * * *

My mother made a particular new friend at the time called Freda Bond. Mrs Bond was Australian and lived with her very English husband, John, in a modern detached house on the main road, one of a row not far from the entrance to the farm lane. Their children, Wendy and Brian, were nearer to my age and also went to boarding school. Our families became friendly and Wendy most generously lent me many of her school stories to read. Wendy also had a small fat pony which I envied her. I would have loved to ride, but when I asked my parents they told me they couldn't afford the lessons, so I didn't ask again as they were so good to me.

After some time my mother found a local job. She had always been an excellent cook and she joined Bena Parsons at a restaurant called the White House, a large attractive black and white building in Henley High Street. My mother worked with Miss Parsons in an old half-timbered building that stood behind the main restaurant. It was called the Bakehouse. They specialised in making scones and cakes to a very high standard and were well-known for this.

66

Bena was in charge. She was an energetic rather plain lady with a sharp voice and manner. She was always humorous and pleasant with me. My mother became very fond of her.

Bena had a brother called Hugh who lived with his wife Faith just outside Henley where he had a stud farm breeding beautiful horses. Bena lived there too. Hugh was wiry, sharp, and very much an outdoors man, tanned and fit and passionately involved with horses. His wife, Faith, was one of the most truly beautiful women I had encountered. She was quite large and dreamy with a profusion of loosely bound up dark auburn hair. She had lovely skin and eyes. Her voice was beautiful, low and musical. I think she was Irish. Her clothes seemed 'floaty' and were quite long, her movements languorous. She had a little son who was very attached to her and not at all interested in the outdoor life as far as I could see.

Perhaps because I was growing older I was interested in all these new adults in my life as well as interested in meeting new children.

Apart from the Bakehouse, The White House also had a kitchen inside the restaurant building where lunches were prepared. It was rumoured that some of the village kitchen staff arrived with flat leatherette shopping bags each day and went home at the end of the day with these same bags bulging with filched kitchen supplies. Food was not rationed in the same way for restaurants, as far as I could understand. Mrs Webster, a lady of considerable mature charms in the style of famed singers and actresses of the day, was the owner of the White House at the time of these depredations. I remember once or twice seeing her floating about during the morning in glamorous satin housecoats at the top of the stairs and would guess she was not very conversant with the business side of the establishment.

I loved going to the White House. My mother went there to work several days a week. While she was there during the mornings if I was home for the holidays I would do a bit of housework in the flat to help out. Sometimes I would then cycle down to the White House and have my lunch in the dining room. One morning I was actually allowed to help make about eighty scones. They were mixed in a small well-scrubbed tin bath. My mother supervised and instructed me and I loved it. My mother enjoyed cooking so much that I wanted to have a go myself and have enjoyed cooking ever since. Ingredients for all the cakes they made were stored in spotless dustbins. One was full of large chunks of cooking chocolate for making butter icing. There was a delicious smell of baking and it was all in great contrast to the rather more meagre meals and food supplies we were used to in the war.

My mother must have found it harder to produce meals for us now that Grandpa was not there providing endless fruit and vegetables for us. I remember seeing my usually good natured mother return from Henley flushed with annoyance at various altercations about distribution of supplies at the greengrocers shop. We began to have rabbit stew which we all enjoyed. Rabbits were not rationed and probably much easier to obtain on the farm. Later in the year my father and I often went out to gather beautiful fresh mushrooms in the fields to eke out our meagre bacon ration for breakfast. Everyone went blackberrying and ate a good deal of Birds custard, Spam and corned beef.

After a while my father joined the Henley division of the Observer Corps. They had an observation post built on the top of the 'mount', one of the highest points for some way round. They were part of a countrywide network.

Using plotting devices the observer corps team had to track the position of enemy aircraft and then immediately relay this information to RAF fighter command and appropriate authorities. This work, part of the country's air defence, also enabled air raid warnings to be given before enemy aircraft were sighted, saving many lives.

My father was very pleased to be doing this work. He made friends among the group of men in the team and felt that he was now more directly involved in the war effort.

His first task was to learn to recognise the silhouettes of both British and enemy aircraft. He was lent a stack of cards, each with the black shape of the plane silhouette on one side, its name on the back. Some of the images were very distinctive but others very similar with only small differences between them. At night time these black shapes would be very difficult to spot against the night sky.

I helped to test him as he learnt to recognise the different planes. We would sit opposite each other in the living room and I would hold up the cards one at a time for him to identify. I could see the names on the back. It was exciting as he quickly learnt them all.

I don't know if there were any observers during the day. As far as I know all of the men had full time occupations and so their spells of duty were after or before their working day.

One very early Summer morning, as my father cycled quietly back up the lane to the farm, there was a faint dawn light in the sky at about half past four. He heard a clicking noise by his front wheel and looking down saw in the dim light an old badger trotting beside him, its nails clicking on the tarmac of the lane. They exchanged a friendly glance before the badger veered off into the hedgerow. My father was delighted by this encounter.

I think it was about a year after we moved to the farm that Miss Wenham decided to sell up and move on. Trent and his mother left too. I was told later that the Ministry of Agriculture was urging farmers to grow more food stuffs and to plough up some of their pastures. Dairy herds were encouraged but beef cattle and sheep were less wanted now. Perhaps that is why Miss Wenham left, as sheep were her main interest.

At first, when we heard that the farm was to be sold, we were alarmed, but then reassured that the new owners would be required to continue with us as tenants, although the change was disturbing.

We were very lucky. The new owners turned out to be Mr & Mrs Whitehouse and their three little boys. Michael the oldest was perhaps about seven, Ian was a toddler and Piers a baby. Mr Whitehouse looked like Bernard Miles, dark and humorous. I think he had a factory or business in Birmingham. His wife, Mrs Whitehouse was a delight to me. Tall, slim and charming she was the first woman I had met who had been to Art School. I liked to talk to her. The Whitehouse's became 'Jack' and 'Phyl' to my parents and they used to meet for drinks together some evenings. We all enjoyed each other's company.

The Whitehouses turned the farm into a large comfortable home for their family. They installed a modern bathroom and kitchen and made various alterations while still keeping the character of the old building. They rented all the farm buildings and fields to other farmers so that the cycle of farming seasons and activities continued exactly as before around us.

Although I still spent time reading and drawing or playing indoors Michael Whitehouse and I began to spend time together, roaming about the land belong to the farm, as Trent and I had done. We would play on the haystacks and cornricks and climb on the old haycart in the rick yard. This cart was old and weathered, springy and somehow welcoming. Michael and I did no damage and respected the farm and its environs. Sometimes we were taken to see new born calves in the stable block. They were very pretty and appealing but I did not like the hot sickly smell of new birth that clung to them. I preferred them a few weeks later as they grew bigger. One day we turned our attention to a little lean-to building outside the back of the red brick barn where cars and bicycles were kept. In Miss Wenham's day ferrets had been kept in the little building, now it was empty except for lumber. I remember we were very keen to turn it into a den for ourselves and were given permission as no one wanted it. We worked hard to clear and tidy it, sweep the floor and clean the windows, but then lost interest once it was completed.

One morning I came across Michael making a fire in a little brick built kiln on the rough ground at the back of the farm. I think his father must have helped him build it. We made clay balls from the soft clay edging the pond and I think we tried to fire them in the kiln. Michael was very practical and good with his hands. I began to think of him almost as a younger brother.

The Whitehouses had a small black and tan terrier called Sal. She was intelligent and affectionate and often came with us on our wanderings.

A place where Michael and I often went to explore was the 'cutting'. An old narrow disused railway line ran diagonally across two fields at the back of the farm. The rails had been removed, just leaving the raised bed of the track which then ran between the steep sides of a railway cutting, a deep notch cut into the steep hillside for past trains to continue on their level way

Buckley Green Farm

The cutting was fenced off from the farm animals but the open wooden rail fence was no barrier to Michael and I who loved to explore the cutting. We made an exciting slide down one of the steep sides, found rabbit holes, bushes, nests, wild flowers and a profusion of butterflies and insects. We didn't venture very far along the track which we had been told ran on to Lapworth, quite a few miles away between farms and fields.

Near to the cutting, towards the top of the hillside, stood two clumps of large horse chestnut trees. One had several chunky wooden square blocks nailed onto the trunk making footholds until you could pull yourself up into the lower branches. I think these blocks had been nailed on by boys who had lived on the farm previously. Once, out on my own, I climbed into this tree and found a comfortable perching place where several branches grew out from the tree trunk. Contained within the bell of green leaves, leaning against the friendly tree trunk I felt that this was my 'special place', comforting and familiar. I always went to 'my' tree on my own.

This tree offered continual seasonal pleasures which I enjoyed during the time we lived at the farm. In the spring creamy blossoms attracted bees, in autumn glossy brown conkers fell in profusion onto the ground. In winter the branches threshed in windy gales. Once my mother, invited to come and visit my tree, watched me climb carefully almost to the top and wave to her below. I could see her figure made small by distance and see the farm and its fields spread out below.

Weekly boarding at the Croft

Since moving to the farm, my weekly boarding at the Croft had been proceeding throughout as usual. Several other pupils travelled from Henley on the train to Stratford Station, then walked together to school. One friendly day girl was the daughter of the family who ran Henley's famous ice cream parlour in the High Street. We envied her close proximity to the delicious ice cream.

Back at school at about this time I began to experience some problems with maths. For some reason I had not learned all my multiplication tables and I think this was a major factor in my slowness and lack of progress. The maths teacher was a sarcastic woman who looked a little like an annoyed Queen Elizabeth the first. She told me in no uncertain terms that I was mentally lazy. She could see that I did well in other subjects and thought I was just not bothering to try in maths lessons. Under her criticism I became nervous and began to dread the lessons. My mind became a blank, although I tried really hard to concentrate. She then began a new routine. The older boarders went to the classroom near matron's office each evening to do their 'prep' supervised by one member of staff. When it was the math's teacher's turn she used to summon me from the playground or playroom where the younger pupils were spending time before getting ready for bed. She would make me stand in front of her and then in front of the older girls would ask me questions which involved knowing my tables. As I grew used to this

routine I would go to the cloakroom to cry before our encounter as I was absolutely determined not to cry in front of her. I would try desperately to answer her, but with little success. The older girls doing their homework looked uncomfortable as these interrogations progressed. Sometimes they would try to whisper the correct answers to me. Perhaps one of them complained to another member of staff. Quite abruptly these tormenting sessions ceased.

Why it had never entered my head that my troubles would be over if I learned all my multiplication tables thoroughly, I simply cannot imagine. I'm sure that if Miss Porter had been teaching maths she would have directed me and encouraged me to do so however long it took me. Perhaps the maths teacher was right and I was just lazy, and surely rather dim not to have worked out how to make life easier for myself.

Another lesson that I disliked was French, but here I am ashamed to say that in this case I was one of the tormentors and not the tormented.

For these French lessons we had a small elderly teacher with dark shingled hair. Something in her manner, a mixture of nervousness and uneasy bluster very gradually brought out the bully in all of us. We began to be cheeky and difficult and to sense our power as she became more and more visibly agitated.

73

Once she sent me to stand outside the classroom door for some misdemeanour. After a while, standing on the dark landing, I heard the voices of Miss Phillips and Matron coming closer. If Miss Phillips found me standing outside the door I would be doubly admonished. Against the wall were rows of coats on pegs where some of the day girls hung up their things on reaching school. It had been raining that morning and Wellingtons were in neat rows standing beneath the coats. Holding my shoes in my hand I slipped my feet into a pair of tall Wellingtons and eased my way against the wall behind the damp coat hanging above. I was completely concealed except for a gap where the coat did not meet the top of the Wellingtons. The landing was dark and the whole area poorly lit. With beating heart I stood perfectly still and prayed that I would not sneeze or cough.

Miss Phillips and Matron paused on the landing to discuss something to do with sheets and laundry. Even in the midst of my panic I was surprised to hear Miss Phillips sounding very pleasant and ordinary. Perhaps in her role as headmistress in front of the pupils she felt she had to present a more severe aspect in order to impose discipline. Eventually, still chatting, they moved away and I left my damp hiding place with relief.

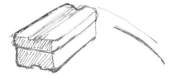

When our rebellion became more open and defiant the French teacher became more agitated with every lesson. Once she threw the blackboard rubber at a pupil. Not long after that she sat crouched

74

over her table, her mouth working and making strange sounds, close to tears. At this point a general embarrassment and shame overcame us. With unspoken accord we settled down and began to work at last. We never misbehaved in French lessons again.

While Miss Porter, her friend Miss Thompson and Miss Phillips were there throughout my years at the Croft, other teachers came and went.

Miss Robinson wore her grey hair plaited and then pinned into whorls over her ears. She was rather stately and mild, and taught us a great deal about nature study which we enjoyed. No one ever misbehaved in her class.

A very pleasant woman came in to teach elocution. I think in our eyes she was a woman like our mothers and their friends and not exactly a teacher. Some of the older pupils took elocution exams after much coaching. Our elocution teacher told them on no account to lose their concentration or poise WHATEVER happened. Apparently on one occasion the examiner had crawled about under his desk retrieving papers to put off the pupil as she recited her poems. Forewarned of eccentric behaviour she had carried on regardless, earning high marks.

Our singing teacher, another visitor to the school, was literally larger than life. Of considerable girth and exuberant presence Mrs Gilkes swept in and out of our lives in voluminous garments and a cloak, her rich voice and dramatic gestures commanding our attention.

While we all took part in the singing lessons I think the elocution lessons were a paid extra. My parents probably thought that elocution might be useful to countermand any lingering village speech mannerisms, but they were rather more uncertain about my desire to learn to play the piano. They were right to be dubious. Tone deaf and almost unable to sing a simple song in tune, my progress at music was painfully slow. I remember that after some weeks the scale of C, and one very short repetitive tune, were all that I could muster. Each evening I was sent to practice for half an hour in a room beneath the senior prep room. One evening an anguished senior came down from above, to plead 'Could you please play something else or kindly STOP! How happy I was when it was decided that these lessons should come to an end. Apparently when consulted by my parents, Miss Phillips had remarked 'Gillian's piano playing will certainly not set the Thames on fire'. For once I was grateful to her.

Looking back I think my problems with maths and music and French *were* due to laziness. I enjoyed English, History, Scripture, Geography and so on because I was interested in the subject matter. What I did not enjoy was rote learning, either of multiplication tables, music notation or the tenses of French verbs. I was too short sighted to understand that if I mastered this early rote learning I would then progress with more speed and understanding. So easy to be wise in hindsight.

* * * * *

Miss Porter's friend, Miss Thompson, was in charge of the infants. Where Miss Porter was of medium height and stockily built, Miss Thompson was tall and slim with dark hair and a very pleasant light melodious voice. Even as children we were aware that they were great friends as they would often pause and talk and laugh together. We all liked Miss Thompson although she never taught us, being busy with the infants. We used to see the small boys and girls going in and out of their building. They didn't use our playground. We went across to the Infants hall to do PE. There was a raised stage at one end and here Miss Porter stood energetically demonstrating all the physical exercises for us to copy. This hall had a smooth polished wooden floor and the room was sunny and felt happy and pleasant. I liked the large pinned up paper illustrations – pictures of rosy cheeked children gathering apples in impossibly lovely orchards for example – sentimental in the manner of the day but very well drawn. They were probably from the magazine Teachers World which I came across years later.

In this room we were also taught dancing and I can remember some breathless sessions with much smiling and laughing as we learnt to dance the polka.

Here too, yearly plays were put on. These were enacted by senior girls but once I had a non-speaking part in one of them. Another junior girl named Janet and I were chosen because we were of similar height and build and both had straight fair hair. We were chosen to play two angels in a performance of Milton's 'Comus' We had long white gowns, golden halos and bare feet. I particularly remember the bare feet as it was so cold standing behind the canvas back drop waiting to go on. We then had to stand angelically on either side of some steps while the actors declaimed and moved about. The plot went straight over my head, I concentrated on trying not to move as my icy toes smarted unbearably.

At one of these winter performances, sometime previously, Miss Phillips had gone up on to the stage to welcome the packed audience of parents and governors. Apparently she had somehow stepped into and knocked over one of the fire buckets concealed at the side behind the stage curtain. The icy water was precipitated onto the laps of the seated governors in the front row. This story had passed into legend. If it was true in every particular I am not sure, but we all enjoyed it so much that it was frequently repeated.

* * * * *

Our daily after school walks were varied. They usually left the town by the quieter streets and led us into the countryside. One favourite walk began by going along the 'tramlines', a raised tarmaced walkway where many years previously an ancient little horse-drawn tram had run from Stratford out alongside the Shipton road. Sometimes we walked beside the river or beside the canal. Occasionally on days of bitter cold and sunshine, sparkling hoar frost outlined every leaf and twig. We enjoyed all the seasonal changes and hoped especially for snow.

During my first winter at the Croft we heard from the day girls that the basin had frozen over into thick ice. This was the canal basin in part of the riverside gardens near the theatre. We were being taken for our walk by a new and inexperienced teacher. We had somehow conveyed to her that we were allowed to walk past the basin. In actual fact we were never taken there. However the new teacher, disarmed by our friendly chatter, allowed us to head decorously two by two towards our goal. On arrival the large expanse of ice and the groups of sliding children enchanted us. Within moments we were on the ice. Among groups of youths and local children we launched ourselves down glittering slides with frenzy. Decorously clad in our navy school coats and velour hats, held on firmly by elastic under the chin, we zipped past the distraught teacher who stood on the path beseeching us to come off. With sparkling eyes and red cheeks we savoured our short freedom turning a blind eye to the teacher's exhortations. Then, almost as if at a given signal, we climbed back onto the path. On the way back to school we all arrived at the unspoken decision that no one would mention this sliding back at school and that this reticence was to include the teacher. And so it was. No reprimand followed. The new teacher became more experienced and firmer with us. We bore her no malice but remembered that brief freedom with delighted glee and satisfaction

* * * * *

All mealtimes at the Croft started with the grace 'For what we are about to receive may the Lord make us truly thankful'. After grace we all sat down together. The mistress in charge of each of the three tables of pupils would supervise table manners. No one started eating until everyone had been served. No one was allowed to ask for anything. Neighbours kept an eye on you and asked for water or bread or condiments to be passed to you. You reciprocated by looking after them. I don't remember anyone ever leaving any food on any occasion.

Just occasionally there would be a lovely surprise. The whisper would go round before we got to the dining room – 'Oranges today'. When we went into breakfast there on each of the polished dark wooden tables would be large bowls of oranges, a brilliant splash of colour. Then the room would fill with their unique perfume. The oranges were always large and sweet, a wonderful treat.

If it was your birthday during term time you were allowed to have your birthday cake on your particular table if parents had delivered one to school. At supper time, once it was carefully cut up into small pieces by the teacher, you offered a piece to the others on your table. Then it had become a tradition that you carried it to the staff dining table.

Cakes were hard to come by during the war. My mother always sent large splendid cakes she had made herself. At my request they were often feather light sponge cakes, one palest pink, one eau de nil and one cream coloured. They were sandwiched together with butter cream and then iced. I felt very proud as I carried my offering to the staff table where I was greeted by more than usual graciousness.

At morning break when we flocked down to the dining room for a glass of milk, the boarders were given their letters. As for most of the time at the Croft I was a weekly boarder my need for letters was not as great as that of the termly boarders. Despite that I had a letter every Wednesday. This was almost always from my father in his flowing hand. He was the letter writer of our family and sent informative and affectionate letters. How unjust then that my mother's letters, sent rarely, should be received with such delight, while my fathers were almost taken for granted. In contrast to my father's elegant handwriting, my mother's writing was what I called 'fat writing'. It was bold, large, rounded and vigorous. Her letters were also bound to be brief, but much treasured.

The playroom was one of my favourite rooms at the Croft, the scene of much enjoyment. We thought it was just a square darkish old room situated to the right of the front door as you

79

came in up the steps. Thinking back to its wooden panelling, walls of built-in bookshelves, its window seats and wooden shutters I think it was probably still one of the least altered rooms in the old house.

In the summer our after supper playtime often took place in the outside playground, but on colder, darker days the playroom was used. It was heated by a glowing stove and was warm and comfortable however cold the weather.

Here we had much fun, probably because we were quite often unsupervised for much of the time. We used to play the game of 'murder' which was organised by one or two of the older juniors. I suppose the seniors must have had their own version of our playroom as I don't remember any of them being with us.

These older girls had dormitories right at the top of the building and perhaps they had a sitting room up there. Once, for a dare, I made my way round the playroom hanging onto the bookshelves, placing my feet on the little wooden ledge at the base of the bookcase doors about four feet from the ground. The shelf cracked and creaked ominously so I didn't try again.

On another occasion we broke the sofa. We had placed the old sofa end on in the middle of the room. We lined up facing one end, then in turn ran forward, somersaulted over the arm and thumped down full length on the sofa seats before bouncing up to join on the end of the line once more. At the height of our enjoyment when the poor old sofa had already taken much punishment, as a fairly hefty pupil hurled herself over the arm yet again the entire side of the sofa fell off onto the floor.

We were horrified. We stood round in consternation. At this point some member of staff came in. I have no memory of Miss Phillips being involved or any kind of punishment. Maybe what happened was so awful that I have blacked out the memory. Or maybe the sofa was already so old and damaged that no blame was apportioned. We rarely told tales and I don't think any adult could have known that we had been playing so wildly. We were supervised for most of the day, a wise precaution, because we were young and healthy and many of us were full of mischief. We simply did not have enough outlet for our physical energy or our own initiatives.

A time which irked us a good deal was time spent in bed after lights out. We were sent to bed quite early each night. After the rituals of washing and changing and preparing for bed Matron would come round to say goodnight and put out the lights. In winter time there always seemed to be someone with a chesty cough who had to drape a towel over their head and inhale Friars Balsam. That unpleasant smell always takes me back to those days.

If it was cold and dark we were often quite glad to snuggle down in our beds. I don't remember any form of heating in the bedrooms. Talking was strictly forbidden after lights out. We never obeyed the rule but conversed in whispers, alert for the footfall of any patrolling teacher. Once, quite late outside our door, we heard a teacher call out, 'Have you heard the news, Leslie Howard is dead, we just heard it on the news'. We knew Leslie Howard was a film star and were surprised to hear teachers sounding so upset.

It was the long light summer evenings that were so trying. The light was bright behind the thin curtains and we were bored and not sleepy. Outside in the sunny street someone went by whistling on a bicycle. We would get out of bed and practice handstands and walking on our hands round the room. Someone showed us how to stand on top of our beds, feet pointing toward the end of our bed, almost touching the iron bedstead at the foot. The idea was then to dare to fall backwards onto our bed, not bending at all, keeping our body rigid, arms straight by our sides, ending up with our head on the pillow. This was difficult and therefore admired. We took it in turns to watch each other try. The iron bedsteads complained badly but never broke. After a time we tired of this.

Once a particular friend and I had a craze for making woolly balls. Our wool blankets were thin, coloured fawn with a coloured stripe at each end. Patiently we would pluck fluff from our blankets, bit by bit, until we had a little ball. The most prized balls were those made from the coloured stripe. We secreted these in a tall vase in the bedroom. No one ever found out, although I suppose Matron must have been puzzled by our ever more threadbare blankets. If I could have had books, paper and pencils I would have been as good as gold. As it was our extreme boredom gave rise to these strange activities until we were tired enough to sleep.

Once at playtime one of the older pupils took me aside and related to me the story of how babies were made. It sounded pretty outlandish to me. Why this older pupil told me I have no idea. I think she had just acquired this information and was dying to tell some else. That night, in dramatic whispers, I regaled my dormitory with this startling information, adding a few embellishments of my own. Heaven knows how many of them were blighted by my imaginative additions.

For my tenth birthday, rather to our joint surprise, I had asked my mother for a bible. My father's present would be given to me at the weekend. My birthday fell midweek in June and on the day itself I was told that a little parcel had been delivered for me at Matron's office. I went along and was given my parcel and a bunch of beautiful fragrant roses. To my astonishment I was given a vase and allowed to have the roses in my dormitory. No one had ever had fresh flowers in their room before. My mother had asked Kay, a young friend of hers, to deliver my parcel as she lived in Stratford. I discovered later that Kay had also delivered the bunch of roses from her own garden. For some reason I was also allowed to keep my new bible in my room, and I remember waking early on light summer mornings and sitting up to read it.. The thin pages were crisply printed and there were plenty of lovely coloured illustrations. I enjoyed the dramatic stories and particularly the language.

As the roses gradually let slip their petals I collected some crimson ones and pressed them between the pages of the bible so that for many years the book held a gentle fragrance and memories of the surprise and pleasure of that far off birthday.

Henley Holidays

Henley Holidays

Early on next summer I caught glandular fever. We heard that another girl who lived not far along a nearby lane had caught it too. Apparently the doctor thought this might have been because we had both drunk milk from the same source. If this was correct or not I don't know, but I remember my mother talking about this at the time. As usual she made no fuss but looked after me and was very kind and comforting. I spent most of my time in my parents' big bed in their airy bedroom. I suppose they must have slept in the twin beds in my room! My cat was allowed to sleep on the foot of the bed which would not previously have been permitted, but Minna seemed to know I was ill and was a great comfort. I remember little about the illness except that I felt weak and hot and had a very high temperature and pounding headaches.

I do remember very clearly hearing the doctor say, as I recovered, 'Don't send her back to school, let her have the whole of the rest of the summer off to build up her strength'. I could hardly believe it – wonderful.

Much later I heard that the other girl had died and was shocked and very sorry. Perhaps this accounted for mysterious sounds I had heard one evening when I was still very ill. It sounded like my mother crying quietly in the other room, and my father comforting her. As I had never seen or heard my mother cry and as both my parents were always cheerful in front of me I had almost convinced myself that I had dreamed the crying episode.

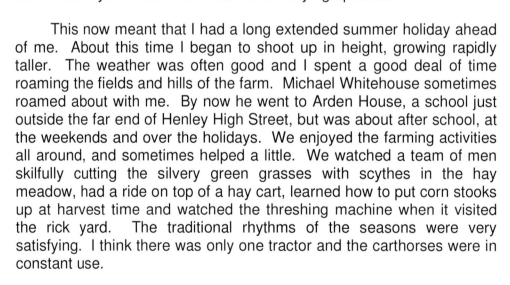

This now meant that I had a long extended summer holiday ahead of me. About this time I began to shoot up in height, growing rapidly taller. The weather was often good and I spent a good deal of time roaming the fields and hills of the farm. Michael Whitehouse sometimes roamed about with me. By now he went to Arden House, a school just outside the far end of Henley High Street, but was about after school, at the weekends and over the holidays. We enjoyed the farming activities all around, and sometimes helped a little. We watched a team of men skilfully cutting the silvery green grasses with scythes in the hay meadow, had a ride on top of a hay cart, learned how to put corn stooks up at harvest time and watched the threshing machine when it visited the rick yard. The traditional rhythms of the seasons were very satisfying. I think there was only one tractor and the carthorses were in constant use.

I saw a good deal of my cat Minna this summer. In many ways she was quite independent, sleeping in the farm buildings at night and spending time hunting mice in the barns and long grass. If my parents and I were out for small walks in the light summer evenings down the lane or particularly in the fields, she would come with us, either well behind us or suddenly racing ahead. When we caught up with her she would look at us in feigned surprise as if to say 'Fancy seeing you here'.

Early one damp, misty summer morning I decided to go further along the disused railway line where Michael and I had occasionally explored before. Leaving the cutting behind the track now continued between quiet farmland, sometimes between grassy banks, sometimes raised above the surrounding fields. There was one pretty bank where violets grew in spring, followed in summer by tiny wild strawberries. I began to jog along a stretch of line where bushes grew part way across the track, so I had to brush back the branches so as to get through.

Suddenly my feet were squelching through something, glutinous and rubbery, not the grass of the track. Looking down I saw in one horrified glance that I was running through a broad swathe of large silvery slugs who were crossing the track.

I was already too far into the broad rippling band of slugs to go back. With shudders and gritting my teeth I squelched on to gain the grass again. I was upset because I had trodden on so many and must have hurt them. I felt sick and brushed my sandaled feet against grassy tussocks to clean them. The slugs, hundreds of them, continued on their way. I went further and found tiny, crimson strawberries, but even they could not put right the morning. Warily I went back. To my great relief the slugs were gone. Where they had all been going in such numbers remained a mystery.

That year I was particularly aware of the beautiful wildflowers. perhaps because I had so much extra time to look at them.

Earlier, before I was ill, I had been transfixed by the sudden blossoming of bluebells. Along the lane to Mobb's farm, a border of young trees was carpeted by a sheet of their hyacinth blue flowers, glowing intensely, seeming to give off an exquisite aura of perfume and shimmering colour. I picked some and took them up to the flat where they immediately drooped and looked disappointingly sad. In future I enjoyed them where they bloomed and never picked them.

That same lane was partly lined by dog-roses in the summer and by blue periwinkle flowers growing in Miss Findon's hedge.

There were few poppies in the harvest fields but the tiny red flowers of scarlet pimpernel grew at the base of the corn stalks. One of the best places for wild flowers was the little triangular meadow at the side of the farm. Here I enjoyed the cool pale mauve flowers of lady's smock and especially the exotic patterned bells of snakes head fritillaries. I don't think this field had ever been cultivated. This was before the time of pesticides and crop spraying so bees and wild flowers flourished.

During the holidays I quite often saw Wendy and Brian Bond and once Norma came to stay. I think she found the countryside rather daunting. It took me some time to realise this. Because I loved climbing trees I assumed she would too. I once goaded her into climbing into a small wild pear tree and then had the greatest difficulty in helping her to climb down again. After this I became more thoughtful about our joint activities so that she could enjoy herself too.

During Norma's visit to the farm I heard how very different their life was back in Birmingham, where bombing was heavy and frequent in parts of the city. For all this time they had slept in the air raid shelter that Uncle Ralph had had excavated deep beneath their house. It was not comfortable and was damp so that the bedding had to be dragged upstairs every day to be aired. Norma's mother, Aunty Hilda, had bronchitis each winter which was aggravated by this time in the shelter.

Uncle Ralph did air raid warden duty. Once, while helping people from a bombed building, the wardens were 'strafed' by enemy planes returning from their bombing missions in the city.

Not many houses were destroyed in Moseley itself where they lived, but water mains were destroyed which meant they had to fill their bath with cold water and use it very sparingly until water pipes were restored. Queues and shortages seemed much worse in the towns than the country.

Nevertheless Norma told us they still enjoyed themselves. People made their way through the blackout in the evenings to each others houses, sharing their rations and having impromptu parties.

Throughout the War people listened to the radio on and off every day. Primarily everyone listened to the daily news bulletins but various comedy shows and regular programmes of entertainment were very popular. I had listened avidly to Children's Hour for years, but now began to take an interest in drama programmes. Jane Eyre was dramatised in weekly serial form and I found it intensely exciting, dramatic and mysterious. My parents would call me in from play so that I didn't miss a minute of any episode. Mr Rochester became a great hero and I loved the story.

The cinema too was heavily patronised during the war and I sometimes went with my parents to 'the pictures' at the Stratford cinema. Everyone smoked in those days and the cinemas were packed with no empty seats. I still enjoy watching black and white films from that era as they bring back the atmosphere of the time so vividly.

As a family we went to Stratford during the school holidays quite often, partly because my father now had a job just outside Stratford. He worked for a firm which sold small wooden greenhouses. I think they were the first to sell pre-packed parts of greenhouses which could be easily transported and then assembled on site. As everyone was growing more and more of their own food this innovative design did well. The firm always had a stand at agricultural shows. I visited these shows with my father or both parents and loved being among so many animals. These shows seemed to take place despite the war.

We spent every Christmas with Granny and Grandpa Goodenough at the Firs at Tredington which was a joy to us all, and often saw Granny Emett too.

Later America came into the war and we began to see Americans about in Stratford. The smooth cloth of their uniforms, their drawling voices and cigars gave them a relaxed appearance. Some of Uncle Fred's Punch cartoons began to feature these new allies.

"... guess we should have forked RIGHT at the traffic-lights."

Although I don't remember seeing them anywhere other than at Stratford my parents once had an amusing encounter with an American soldier. They were driving in their little car behind a large American supply lorry down a narrow Warwickshire lane. Because the lane was so narrow they could not pass. Sitting in the back of the lorry, facing them, was an American GI. They all smiled at one another. After some time the American soldier picked up a large tin from a pile beside him, pointed at the tin, pointed at my parents, grinned and then threw the tin into the soft grasses of the ditch at the side of the lane. Then, with a thumbs up sign he was trundled away round a corner. Stopping the car and getting out to investigate my parents found to their delight a very large tin of pineapple chunks. This was untold luxury at a time when our war time rations were so monotonous and meagre. They bore the tin home in triumph and gratitude.

About this time I developed mysterious dry patches on my forehead and upper arms. The doctor suggested that we should consult a skin specialist in Birmingham. My mother and I made a visit one dark wintry day. I was amazed to see the bomb damage as our bus travelled towards the centre of the city. Small houses had been ripped apart, leaving the pathetic details of half demolished rooms and staircases exposed to view. There were large bomb sites and in the city centre itself strange gaps where stores, offices and imposing buildings had stood previously. Everyone went about their business briskly as usual and any areas of destruction had been swept and tidied or enclosed behind hoardings.

The specialist had upstairs rooms in a tall dignified building looking up Corporation Street. Marble and mahogany were in evidence as we sat in the large gloomy waiting room.

At one point during our wait I heard the loud sound of horses hooves, jingling harness and the rumble of cart wheels. I darted to the window to look out. There coming down steep Corporation Street, was a large brewers dray laden with barrels and pulled by four splendid dray horses. This sight enlivened my day. The smartly painted dray, the proud carter and the glossy horses all breathed defiance at dreary war time proceedings.

When we were called in, after talking to my mother for some time, the consultant asked me to sit still below a bright light while he looked at my skin through a very large magnifying glass. Seeing his own eye hugely magnified as he examined me I felt a faint desire to giggle, but quelled it immediately.

One of the results of the visit was that I was found to be suffering from a vitamin deficiency. From then on I was prescribed yeast tablets at each meal and vitamin C in the form of government orange juice, fresh fruit where possible and blackcurrant Ribena. These measures worked and my skin improved after a few weeks. As the yeast tablets tasted rather strange on their own I developed a trick of inserting them sideways into pieces of bread or toast where I quite enjoyed them.

During this time of food shortages, country people continued with their usual practice of foraging for wild food, so we did too. My father and I carried on looking for mushrooms wherever possible, and everyone went blackberrying and searched for hazelnuts in the hedges. Occasionally a wild damson tree would be found and was then stripped to make jams and pies. Rose hips were collected for the Women's Institute for making rose hip syrup. Some people made crab apple jelly.

* * * * *

One winter we had a sudden fall of thick snow. My father was about, it must have been the weekend, and he and I went out with my sledge which had been built for me by my Uncle Eric just before the war. It was strong and light, a lovely shape. We took it to a steep field behind the farm on the farm's land, part way to Mobb's farms. It was tiring to climb the steep hillside in the thick snow. We got hot in the thick extra clothing we were wearing. Once we pushed off we had a most wonderful swift descent to the bottom. It must have been getting on for tea time. The sun was a crimson disc, very low in the wintry sky. We had time for several climbs and glorious descents before it began to get dark. Holding the rope for the sledge we took it in turns to drag the sledge back up the hill. Once my fingers were so frozen that the rope slipped from my hands and I didn't notice until we turned and saw the sledge gently gliding down by itself to the bottom. After one more go we went back to the warm farmhouse climbing up the steep little stairway to my mother and tea.

90

Holy Trinity Church, Stratford on Avon

Termly Boarding at the Croft

Well before the end of my time at the Croft Jennifer left and I became friendly with a new girl called Ann Crespi. Ann was dark haired and volatile, rather different from the other girls.

Ann's mother had lodgings quite near the school and I saw her occasionally. She was small but very upright, plump with a regal bearing and soft buttery skin and fair hair. She had a pleasing speaking voice. Ann's father was Italian and her parents had both sung in opera before the war.

To their outrage, because her father was not British, he was interned on the Isle of Man for the duration of the war. I remember Ann's description of soldiers coming suddenly and taking him away in a lorry to their shock and dismay. She told me this in an accusing sort of way as if she held me, together with other British people, as somehow responsible. All this was a surprise to me as I had no idea this went on.

Ann and I shared a small dormitory for two, upstairs over the main porch and entrance to the front door of the school building. Outside our bedroom window was the flat top of the porch, overhung by a flagpole. One hot summer evening we daringly got out onto the porch roof in our pyjamas. The quiet street dozed in the evening calm and rather to our disappointment there was no one there to see us.

Perhaps because Ann told me how much nicer school was at the weekends I asked my parents if I could become a termly boarder and found that there was a much more relaxed atmosphere during the weekends. In the summer we were taken for many interesting new walks and once spent an afternoon blackberrying near the monument. Beetle drives, charades and other games were organised in colder months.

Sometimes I regretted asking to be a termly boarder but in the main I enjoyed it and liked having Ann for a particular friend.

One change that occurred now that I was at school over the weekends was weekly churchgoing. Ann who was a Catholic, and two pretty Jewish girls did not come. The rest of us were taken every Sunday morning to Holy Trinity Church where Shakespeare was buried.

It was a lovely church and I enjoyed looking at the building and particularly liked a small stained glass window showing St Nicholas, the original 'Father Christmas'. I liked the short walk to the church and the smooth, broad old flagstones on the tree lined path leading to the church door

Inside, in winter time, the heating system which caused warm air to rise from the pierced metal grids over the hot pipes exuded a peculiar sour smell of ancient dust.

However it was warm, a great blessing in contrast to the often rather erratic heating of those war-time days. We sat in a block of chairs towards the back of the pews and the main congregation. I enjoyed the hymn singing and some of the sermons if they were not too long. It was interesting to see the people of the town. Occasionally actors would visit, and it was good to be out of school for a change. There was also a certain amount of drama at times, which often included the town beadle, a small pear shaped man of distinctly eighteenth century shape wearing old fashioned costume. In one ceremony he knocked loudly on the church door. He was always involved in processions to and from the church on various occasions.

During one service the 'last post' was played and on Palm Sunday we all had pieces of palm fronds to hold. All these rituals were enjoyed for their variety. The church was always fairly full and the congregation seemed to enjoy all these events.

The downside of all this church going was winter coughs. All of us at one time or another during the winter would contract heavy colds. Colds seemed to affect the entire population in those days. My nightmare was to cope with a church service when I had a persistent cough which occurred towards the end of any cold I caught. We were expected to exert self-control to avoid coughing during the many quiet parts of the service. To this end I devised a strange process of heavy swallowing to try to prevent coughing until we came to the welcome hymn singing which drowned any noise I might be making. Eventually I would emerge into the cold air limp with relief as we made our way back to school.

After church, and before lunch, we gathered together in one of the smaller upstairs classrooms to do some sewing or letter writing. During the war everyone was continually exhorted to 'make do and mend'.

D A R N I N G   A   H O L E

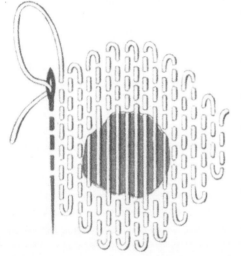

First clear the loops of fluff and broken ends of threads from knitted garments or clip away ragged edges from machine knit fabrics. Always use a darning ball under large holes.

1. Make the darn the shape of the hole.
2. Darn up and down the hole first ; work on the wrong side.
3. Choose mending as fine as the material of the garment.
4. Begin a good distance away from the hole in order to reinforce the thin parts round the hole.
5. Space the rows of darning the width of a strand of mending apart.
6. Pick up the backs of the loops only unless the material is very fine.
7. Leave loops at the ends of each row and darn so that stitches alternate with spaces between stitches in the previous rows.
8. Pick up the edge of the hole in one row then go over the edge of the hole in the next row. If you have cleared the edges of the hole you will find this will be easy and will make a neater mend on the right side of the garment.
9. Continue the darn over the thin place beyond the hole.

Darning over the first rows of darning

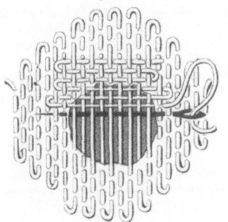

1. Darn over the hole only and about two stitches of darning beyond.
2. Leave loops at the ends of each row, and only pick up on the needle the darning stitches.
3. Pick up the alternate strands of mending in first row.
4. In alternate rows, pick up the strands of mending you passed over in the previous row.

Instruction from a Second World War government leaflet

People wanted to keep their precious clothing coupons for a few particular garments so many learnt how to alter, cut down, reuse, mend, darn and sew existing garments.

One of the kitchen staff named Freda was designated to teach us darning so that we could darn our socks or stockings for ourselves. Freda was plain and not very prepossessing. However her darning was so exquisite that when it was completed it was quite impossible to see where the hole had been. We regarded Freda in a new light. Respectfully we followed her patient demonstrations with determined effort. I enjoyed darning ever afterwards and once astonished my husband twenty years later by invisibly mending a tear in his sports jackets.

* * * * *

For part of our time at the Croft a system of air raid drill was set up. We were asked to bring a large drawstring cotton bag from home. At bedtime we were shown how to put our shoes, socks and all our other clothes neatly into our bags and each put them on our bedside chair. Our dressing gowns were on the back of our chair, our slippers on the floor below.

We practised in daylight at first. At a given signal, we got up quickly and quietly, put on our dressing gowns and slippers, picked up the drawstring bags and lined up at the bedroom door. Then all the dormitories were led down to the dining room. This was a large room, with its roof reinforced by thick timber pillars.

Miss Robinson's plaits!

After a while we had a surprise bomb drill at night. All went as planned and rehearsed and we followed the teacher who had been sent to collect us. To our astonishment when we reached the dining room we saw all the teachers in their dressing gowns and slippers too. To see our headmistress wearing a dressing gown and smiling at us with approval gave us an uneasy feeling. We felt disorientated.

Miss Porter looked much the same, energetic and reassuring in some business-like garment, but the ultimate surprise among the other teachers was Miss Robinson. She had not had time for the laborious pinning of her plaits into whorls over her ears and they hung, long and thin as skipping ropes almost to the floor.

On one other occasion we saw our teachers out of their usual role. In the big downstairs classroom our teachers actually put on a play for us. To our incredulous eyes we saw them as a group of school children, one even riding an outsize tricycle. I think this was probably a clever and witty sketch, but it just made us feel uncomfortable. We felt as though we were watching a private joke. It certainly did not make us like our teachers more. We were all relieved to see them back in role the next day.

* * * * *

Ann and I began to become intrigued by Shakespeare at this point. Older pupils and staff frequently talked about him and the town was full of references to him. The Shakespeare Memorial Theatre stood at the bank of the river Avon and we frequently passed it on our walks or visits to our sports playing fields on the opposite bank.

Shakespeare's school room was only a few hundred yards from ours, his daughter had lived at Hall's Croft in the Old town close to our school and we saw his wife's cottage at Shottery when we walked there to use the tennis courts in summer.

Shakespeare's school room

What particularly aroused my interest were some large very old-fashioned volumes of his plays in the book cases in our playroom. These books had detailed Victorian engravings illustrating all the plays. I especially liked a picture of Puck sitting on a toadstool surrounded by fairies from A Midsummer Night's Dream. We were allowed to look at all these books if we handled them carefully.

Once, during the weekend, we were all taken to a play in the old part of the theatre which was attached to the very modern new theatre. We loved it. Anything to do with the theatre and acting appealed to Ann and I. We found actors flamboyant and interesting. They often had beautiful speaking voices and seemed to us to inhabit a more glamorous world. Our daily walks in Stratford and its environs began to be enlivened by our secret craze of 'actor spotting.' I liked a young Andrew Faulds and Ann was keen on an actor whose first name was Graham.

Ann came to stay at the farm during the summer of 1944. We enjoyed ourselves roaming about the fields, exploring further along the cutting and visiting Henley. My parents took us to Charlecote Park to see the lovely old house and grounds and to the Shakespeare Memorial theatre to see As You Like it. The high spot for us both was going to the cinema with my parents at the Shirley Odeon to see Laurence Olivier in Shakespeare's Henry V.

This innovative and clever film delighted the packed audience. The battle scenes with their strong patriotic message were so stirring that everyone came out afterwards exhilarated and hopeful.

* * * * *

Back at school quite a few of us began to be interested in films and film stars.

For one or two terms we had a different teacher. Ann and I liked her. She was sympathetic and lively. She was younger than many of the other teachers and had dark curly hair. I don't remember her name but I will never forget her for providing us with an unexpected treat.

When we took our walks in crocodile after school the crocodile was led by two experienced older pupils and brought up at the rear by the mistress in charge that day. Two girls were allowed to walk with the teacher. Ann and I asked if we could walk with the new teacher and she said that we may. During the long walk she told us that the film 'Pride and Prejudice' was coming to Stratford cinema and asked us if we knew the story. We had not even heard of Jane Austen, so at our request she told us the plot.

The next Saturday Ann and I were told that we were to be given special permission that afternoon to go to the cinema with our new teacher friend to see Pride and Prejudice. Could this be true? We looked at each other in amazement. Our delight knew no bounds. I think this particular teacher 'lived out' and had offered to take us in her own spare time. What surprised us most was that it smacked of favouritism and we for a change were the favoured! Perhaps we were allowed to go in the interests of literature. Perhaps they were pleased at the prospect of an afternoon without us. That afternoon was heaven to two eleven year old girls, and Darcy became our immediate hero. Sometime later the teacher left, but we never forgot her kindness.

There now began to be rumours about something called the Eleven Plus Exam. Some of us were told that we would be sitting this exam soon. No fuss was made. A group of us were walked to a modern new secondary school to take the exam. I think there were several papers and we may have gone on more than one occasion. What surprised us most was the school building. We sat the exam in a large gymnasium with a gleaming wooden floor. We had never seen a modern purpose built school of this type.

The exams seemed curious. Apart from some of the maths questions which were as baffling as usual, the other questions seemed too easy. One even asked which colour ringed a panda's eyes - black or white? We wondered it there was some hidden agenda as the questions seemed so odd. We returned to school and thought no more about it.

Sometimes at the weekends Ann used to see her mother, who was living nearby, so that they could meet more easily as Ann's father was not there. On one of these occasions a friendly day girl called April had invited me to spend most of one Saturday at her house. This was an enjoyable surprise. April lived in an unusual modern house built entirely of wood near the bottom of Bordon Hill on the outskirts of the town. Her pretty red haired mother who had issued the invitation was Canadian and made me very welcome. During the morning we spent time in a large orchard which abutted their garden among rows of trees in full blossom under the blue sky. It was as lovely as the impossibly pretty orchard illustrations I had seen in the Infants school hall.

Then after lunch April took me to her den beside the front gate in the garden to show me her home-made bow and arrows. In the dry ditch outside her garden hedge she knelt and loosed an arrow across the road, trying to hit a passing car. There were few cars in those days and none of them travelling very quickly. She hit the boot of one car after several tries. Her arrows being homemade from trimmed thin sapling branches did not strike either far or fast and clattered harmlessly off the car whose driver seemed unaware of being a target. As we were kneeling in her den we were hidden from view of any passing motorists.

When it was my turn I knelt down, getting ready to loose an arrow. I aimed at a small van chugging up hill. Just as I released my arrow we heard a sound like an angry hornet and a motor bike sped past on our side of the road. To our horror my arrow hit the petrol tank of the motor bike with a loud clatter and the rider glanced in our direction. We stood up, rooted to the spot. When the motor bike reached the bottom of the hill it stopped and then we heard it coming back towards us.

The burly man who climbed off the bike was a motor cycle policeman! We turned and fled back to April's house. April's mother swiftly took in the situation. She was deferential to the policeman and apologetic without cringing. Sounding reasonable and sympathetic she charmed the policeman to such an extent that he left with just a heavy warning and said that he would, of course, have to contact our school.

Walking back to the school in the summer evening I walked very close to the bulging old red brick garden walls hoping one might fall on me. Compared to the stealing of a few chocolate biscuits which had caused such a furore, what would be Miss Phillips' reaction to hearing that I had shot at a policeman! For the next few days I lived in constant dread. However nothing came of the matter. The policeman had rightly surmised that the threat alone was a sufficient punishment.

*Confessing to my parents at the
Hathaway Tea Rooms*

When my parents took me out to tea the next Saturday I told them what had happened. Their attitude was that I had been very foolish rather than deliberately dangerous and I felt comforted by their usual support and understanding. From then on I became more responsible and felt grateful that I had got off so lightly.

One afternoon, towards the end of the summer term when I was twelve, a teacher stopped me and took me aside. I was told to pack my things ready to leave shortly. I looked at her with complete lack of comprehension. She explained that the school was soon to alter. It had been decided that from now on only Junior School children would be taught at the Croft. All the twelve year olds would be leaving. I was allowed to leave a day or two early at my parents' request as I would have been leaving for the holidays in a short time anyway. I was astounded. I am sure that my parents would have thought that some explanation and plans would have been discussed with me gradually rather than my experiencing this abrupt bombshell.

I discovered later that the reason I was to leave early was so that we could fix up some holiday coaching in maths prior to moving on to secondary school.

I felt bereft. Despite the joy at going home it was a wrench to leave behind all that was so familiar. I found Ann to say goodbye. We were going to stay with each other during the holidays so the parting was not too hard. I remember no farewells to Miss Philips, Miss Porter or any of the other staff. At the time all this was secondary to the excitement of the summer holidays. School was soon forgotten. It is only in later years that this abrupt departure seems so odd.

I know the 1944 Education Act brought about far-reaching changes, but this does not seem to account for the lack of explanation on the part of the school. Perhaps my early departure pre-empted their planned explanations to us all, and perhaps the other pupils were informed of the changes to come in a more considered manner. I'll never know.

* * * * *

Now people began to talk about the end of the war being in sight. VE day had already been celebrated in May earlier in the year. During these summer holidays World War II ended officially with the Japanese surrender on 15 August.

Henley planned to celebrate on top of the 'mount' where beacons and bonfires had been lit to celebrate victories for generations. We climbed up there with a joyful crowd on the day of the festivities, but we decided to leave the wild evening celebrations to the locals whose tradition it was.

In the town below crowds gathered round the old cross in the High Street. One of the events we had been told about was a young people's competition for best decorated bicycles. Keen to enter I had talked to my father about it. As usual he had a good idea. We collected a sheaf of corn from the harvest field by the Dutch barn and tied it onto my bike's handle bars. Then we hung a notice VICTORY HARVEST on the front. This was simple but effective. I was delighted to win the prize for my age group!

Finale

So at last the war was over. I could hardly believe it. That far-off day in our Birmingham kitchen when it had all begun for me seemed so long ago. Then I was a little child, now I was moving towards my teens with different challenges and opportunities ahead. Everyone wondered what the future would hold. Even in the midst of rejoicing some apprehension was felt.

For so many the Second World War had brought problems, desperation, difficulties and bitter loss. I am very aware of how fortunate I was in comparison. For our move from the city to the countryside I have to thank my parents, as for so much else.

I look back in gratitude to my five years in Warwickshire. In this beautiful county I experienced an agricultural way of life that was still unchanged in many ways from earlier times. Later farming gradually became more mechanised and many of the old traditions were lost.

I was grateful too that my war time schooling at the Croft had been so good and equipped me well for my future.

* * * * *

After some time my parents and I left the farm and moved back to Hall Green in Birmingham. I became reunited with Jean and together we attended Solihull High School for girls, remaining friends throughout our lives.

My cousin Norma and I resumed our happy lifelong relationship.

Forty years after the war, when staying in Stratford, my husband and I met Miss Porter and Miss Thompson again and we all became friends. Christmas cards and letters were exchanged and once again I saw that vigorous handwriting that had marked so many of my exercise books long ago

Writing this account of my wartime years has brought back vivid memories, and a recognition that these years enriched my life beyond measure.

Acknowledgements

I am grateful to my friend Jean Wright and my cousin Norma Broom who both refreshed my memory on particular details of this account.

Thanks to my son Matthew who took me back to revisit Halford, Tredington, Stratford and Henley.

Thanks to the painter Hugh Webster and the Tuesday Group at his Felixstowe Ferry Boatshed Studio for their continuous support and encouragement.

Thank you to Sharon Alward at Sharward Services Ltd for her patience and skill.

Thank you to John and Mark at Hot Off The Press Ipswich for 'sizing' my reference material and preliminary drawings.

Thank you to Lyndall Thornton, the present principal of the Croft School, who invited me to the school's 80th Anniversary. The school and I both celebrate our 80th year this June 2013.

Still addicted to tea shops!
Photograph taken by Gill's cousin, Norma, at the Orchard Tea Rooms, Granchester, Cambridge, 2010

Born in 1933 Gill trained initially at Birmingham College of Art in the early 50's and then worked as an illustrator in advertising in Birmingham and in publishing in London.

She married the artist Ray Thomas in 1955 and has two sons.

After a lifetime spent in education she became an advisory teacher for Hampshire County Council and taught for a time at Reading University.

During her retirement in Suffolk Gill studied for her Fine Art degree and gained her BA Hons at Suffolk University in 2008.

She continues to work as an illustrator and painter.

Printed in Great Britain
by Amazon